Walking Round Budapest

Katalin Rohonyi
Miklós Marót

Walking Round Budapest

Corvina

Illustrations by Attila Emődy
Cover design by Mária Hodosi
Cover photo by László Csigó
Translated by Éva Grusz
Revised by George E. Maddocks

© Katalin Rohonyi and Miklós Marót
ISBN 963 13 2695 0

Fourth, revised and enlarged edition

Printed in Hungary, 1988
Kner Printing House, Gyoma
CO 2684-h-8890

Contents

TO THE READER	7
A FEW WORDS ABOUT BUDAPEST	9
A SHORT HISTORY OF THE CITY	11
FINDING ONE'S WAY IN BUDAPEST	18
RECOMMENDED WALKS	19
WALKS	21
1 The Castle District	21
2 The Royal Palace and Its Museums	35
3 The Inner City	39
4 The Parliament Building and Its Neighbourhood	52
5 Gellért Hill and Its Neighbourhood	55
6 The Danube Bank of Buda; Óbuda, Aquincum	59
7 Margaret Island	68
8 Hősök tere (Heroes' Square), the Museum of Fine Arts	71
9 The City Park (Városliget)	76
10 Szent István körút, the Basilica, Népköztársaság útja	80
11 The National Museum, the Museum of Applied Arts	88
WALKS TO SUIT YOUR INDIVIDUAL INTERESTS	93
12 For Lovers of Nature: the Buda Hills	93
13 The Zoological and Botanical Gardens	96
14 For Those Interested in the Subterranean World: the Caves	97
15 For Those Interested in the History of Architecture: Ancient and Historical Monuments	98
16 For Those Who Like Fine Arts and Ethnography	110
17 Budapest for Music-Lovers	115
18 Budapest, the City of Baths	117
19 For Sports Lovers	122

20 Places of Technological Interest	124
21 Szentendre, Visegrád, Esztergom, Nagymaros, Vác	129

PRACTICAL INFORMATION 137

How to Get to Budapest	137
City Transport	138
Travel Offices	139
Accommodation	140
Hungarian Cuisine	143
Night-clubs	
Theatres, Concert halls, and Other Places of Entertainment	146
Museums, Exhibitions	148
Sports	151
Postal Services	151
Newspapers, Journals	152
Shopping	152
Some Important Addresses	154
Sightseeing Tours	155
Recurring Events in Budapest of Interest to Tourists	155
Inscriptions You Will Often See in the City	156

To the Reader

This little book is intended for those who, like you, are able to spend only a few days in Budapest. We feel sure that, whether you are still only planning your tour, or are already here, you want to get to know as much about the city as possible in the short time at your disposal. The aim of this guide is to help you do just that and, at the same time, to suggest ways in which you can plan your programme so as to make the most of your time. Obviously, you cannot even try to see everything! And, as not all the things worth seeing, or all the beauty-spots, are close to one another, we have outlined a series of walks which will take you to those parts of the town, and of its immediate environs, which are of the greatest interest and importance. In this way, we hope, you will be able to form an accurate and vivid general impression of what Budapest has been, and of what it is.

If you are going to spend only one day *in Budapest, you will be able to get an overall view of the city and a glimpse of the old city centre. If you have* two days, *you will, in addition, have time to see what remains from Roman times, the Museum of Fine Arts and some of the medicinal baths.*

In a three days' *programme you should also stroll along the city's loveliest avenue, visit the National Museum and, if the weather is fine, go for a walk in the Buda hills or enjoy the panorama from a pleasure-boat.*

If you are here for four days, *you may like to draw up a programme that suits your own personal tastes: you could go to more of the museums, to one of the frequent exhibitions, look in at some cultural or technical institution, take part in some sport (even if only as a spectator)—or just enjoy yourself.*

If you have five days *in Budapest, we could advise you*

to get to know the environs of the capital, particularly the Danube Bend region lying to the north of the city.

However, if you are going to spend a longer time here, or if you are coming by car and thus have more time for sightseeing, we recommend you to read one of our more detailed guide-books on Hungary and its capital.

We hope that this little book will prove a good adviser and friend to you, and we wish you a pleasant stay in Budapest and lots of happy memories.

A Few Words about Budapest

Budapest, the capital of the Hungarian People's Republic, is situated in the Carpathian Basin, in the heart of the country. A lively city of more than two million inhabitants and the centre of the country's transport, economic, social, scientific and cultural life, it forms a near-circle on both banks of the Danube. The 525 square kilometres (about 200 sq.m.) of its total area are divided into 22 administrative districts. These districts are referred to by the Roman numerals I to XXII, which will be given after addresses in this guidebook.

The city lies in a region of ancient civilization—remains from the Roman and Migration periods, medieval, Renaissance, Turkish, Baroque, neo-Classical, eclectic, Art Nouveau monuments and the most modernistic of buildings can be found side by side in harmony.

The Danube—here 96.5 metres (320 ft.) above sea level—encircles a number of islands north and south of Budapest and also within the area of the city itself, among them the lovely Margaret Island (Margitsziget), a charming park of historical fame. The Budapest stretch of the great river is 28 kilometres (17.5 m.) long, its width varies between 300 and 600 metres (330 and 660 yds.), and its average depth is 3–4 metres (10–13 ft.), which increases to 10 metres (33 ft.) at the Liberty Bridge (Szabadság-híd). Buda, on the right bank, is hilly and wooded, while Pest, on the left bank, lies on the plain. The highest point within the city boundaries, János Hill, is 529 metres (1750 ft.) above sea level. From here, as well as from other nearby hills, an unforgettable view unfolds itself before the spectator.

The climate of the capital is temperate and pleasant. The yearly average temperature is 11°C (52°F), the hottest monthly average is 22°C (72°F) in July, and the coldest, in January, is 1.1°C below zero (30°F). The town is protected from extremes of climate by the surrounding hills. The prevailing north-west wind blows away the polluted air of the town and makes way for the clean air of the Buda Hills. The annual average of 1,991 hours of sunshine is much higher than in most parts of Central Europe.

In the hot summer months the Buda hills, the banks and islands of the Danube and the medicinal baths provide relief from the heat. On sunny autumn and spring days excursions and walks are particularly rewarding, and in winter the hills resound to the gay sounds of those sleighing or skiing.

Budapest is especially rich in medicinal waters. Most of the springs are close to the surface and as early as the Middle Ages they assumed great importance for the water-supply of the town. Others are lukewarm or hot medicinal springs of great curative value, coming from vast depths. Around these there are medicinal baths, medicinal institutions, hotels and swimming-pools for those who are in search of rest or cure in this great city—a city which offers both the entertainments and busy life of a great metropolis and the contrast of relaxing and refreshing walks in quiet woods.

A Short History of the City

The 2000-year history of the whole Carpathian Basin is reflected in the history of Budapest.

Prehistory: In the third century B.C. the Indo-European Illyrian-Pannonian tribes inhabited this area. Their name is preserved in the title of Pannonia (Hungary). This was a decisive period in the history of the Hungarian capital. The Illyrian-Pannonians were followed by the Celts (e.g. Ak-ink=abundant water, Aquincum) arriving from the West, from whom the names of the later Roman settlements were derived. The name of the river Danube also originates from them.

Roman Period: In the first century A.D. the Roman legions occupied the parts of present-day Hungary lying to the west of the Danube and founded—on the site of today's Óbuda (in the northern part of Buda)—Aquincum, the chief town of the province which they called Pannonia. Along the Danube they built a road as well as a defensive border, the *limes,* consisting of watchtowers and fortresses. On the Pest side, too, watchtowers were constructed. In the second century the number of inhabitants totalled 20,000–30,000; at the end of the fourth century, however, when the Roman Empire was already declining, most of the inhabitants left the town.

In the **Migration Period** it was only around the ferry, at the foot of today's Gellért Hill, that more or less permanent settlements grew up on both banks of the river. It is believed (though it is a much disputed question) that the names of Buda (meaning hut, small house) and Pest (meaning cave, recess) are derived from the language of Bulgarian-Slav tribes and can be dated back to this period.

The **Magyar** (Hungarian) **Conquest** took place in the

ninth century; the Magyar tribes, led by Prince Árpád, advanced from the East and settled in the Carpathian Basin around the year 896. As crossing-places of the Danube gained importance, many merchants settled in this area.

The kings of the House of Árpád reigned from the year 1000—the year when the founder of the State, (Saint) Stephen I was crowned—to 1301. At the turn of the tenth and eleventh centuries the Hungarians adopted Christianity; a parish church was built on the foundations of the Roman watchtower in Pest, and a Chapter was set up at Óbuda. The Mongol invasion of 1241 destroyed an already flourishing town. Afterwards a new town was built on the Castle Hill in Buda, and the construction of a royal palace started. Though at that time Buda was not yet the capital, its central situation gave it a special place among Hungarian towns. The Diet was convoked from the thirteenth century onwards on the Field of Rákos, on the outskirts of Pest.

The reign of the Angevin dynasty, of Sigismund and Matthias—the fourteenth and fifteenth centuries were the Golden Age of Buda. The kings of the Angevin dynasty, Charles Robert and Louis the Great, granted many privileges to Buda and ensured the development of the town. In Óbuda a palace was built for the kings' consorts. Sigismund of Luxembourg, Holy Roman Emperor and King of Hungary, had a palace built on Castle Hill near the royal dwelling-tower of the Angevins, which became the royal seat. King Matthias (Corvinus) Hunyadi (1458–1490), Hungary's last national king, continued the building of the palace, and the houses in the civilian town embellished as well. During his strong, centralized reign one of the most brilliant Renaissance royal households in Europe developed in Buda.

The Turkish occupation: In 1526 the Turkish army advancing from the Balkans annihilated the Hungarian army of Louis II at Mohács. The Sultan entered Buda, but soon returned home and it was only in 1541 that he finally occupied the town. From then onwards, about a third of the country, including Buda, was under Turkish rule. The churches were turned into mosques and the only new buildings were a few baths and some defensive works. A decade or so after the Turkish occupation both Buda and Pest looked like shabby oriental towns. In 1686 the united Christian army recaptured Buda, but once again the siege caused terrible devasta-

One-time Buda (after the engraving made in 1493 by Master Wolgemuth for the Schedel Chronicle)

tion. After the recapture of Buda the country became, and remained until 1918, part of the Habsburg Empire.

In the period of Habsburg absolutism, in the early eighteenth century, both Buda and Pest regained their civic rights. Settlers, invited from many countries to replace the population wiped out by the Turks, built a new town; Buda became the centre of state and military administration and Pest a merchant town, in which national fairs were held four times a year. At the close of the century, the Hungarian university also moved to Pest.

By the **first half of the nineteenth century** both towns had outgrown their former boundaries, and the building of suburbs began. Factories were established: mills, distilleries, textile factories and a shipyard. The new parts of Pest were already being laid out according to a town-planning programme. By the 1840s Pest had also become the centre of Hungarian intellectual life. As early as the end of the eighteenth century a national movement had begun under the influence of French Enlightenment and the French Revolution. Its first manifestation, a conspiracy against Habsburg absolutism led by Ignác Martinovics, had been violently crushed. The next wave of the intellectual movement strove for the cultivation of the Hungarian language and the awakening of national consciousness, and it brought about a flowering of literature written in Hungarian. From the 1820s the best sons of the nation were fighting for social, economic and political reforms, and this 'Reform Period'—the whole movement for economic and cultural rebirth, strengthened by the industrialization process—culminated in the revolution of March 1848 and in the War of Independence of 1848–49 against Habsburg absolutism. The most decisive events of these took place in Pest-Buda, as the twin towns were then known.

In the **second half of the nineteenth century** urbanization assumed proportions hitherto unknown in Hungary. Industrialization concentrated the great industries in the capital; in fifty years the population quintupled; an industrial proletariat came into being and workers' suburbs were built around the city. In 1872–73 Pest, Buda and Óbuda became officially united under the name of Budapest, and the first large public buildings—in an eclectic-historical style—were constructed, with districts covered with blocks of flats around them.

The period of the two world wars. The First World

PEST

One-time Pest (19th-century engraving by F. M. Paur)

War brought poverty and misery to the country, above all to the capital. In the autumn of 1918 the Austro-Hungarian Monarchy collapsed, and the Hungarian working class—which had by then become an organized force—brought into being the Hungarian Republic, and on 21 March 1919 proclaimed the Hungarian Republic of Councils. In August 1919, however, owing to the numerical superiority of the counter-revolutionary forces in the country and abroad, the Republic of Councils was defeated and Admiral Miklós Horthy, representing the old régime, assumed power as Regent. During the years of consolidation in the twenties mainly villas and garden suburbs were built, while the masses of the population, workers and other people of low income, continued to live in tenement houses and slums. In 1941 Hungary entered the Second World War on the side of Nazi Germany. In March 1944 the German troops occupied and plundered the country, ruined all the bridges and turned the capital into a battlefield. The Soviet army wiped out the German troops holding Budapest in a siege which lasted from Christmas 1944 to 13 February 1945; they had liberated the whole country by the spring of 1945.

Reconstruction after 1945. As a result of air raids and street fighting 70.2 per cent of the dwelling-houses in Budapest were damaged; 3.8 per cent were completely destroyed. All the Danube bridges were blown up by the German army. In the years following the war the ruins were rapidly cleared and the first task was then to rebuild the railways, the bridges and the factories. In 1946 Parliament proclaimed a Republic and in 1949 Hungary became a People's Republic. The reconstruction of the capital progressed at great speed; in 1950 the suburbs were merged with the capital and the area of Budapest thus became two and a half times larger than before the war.

Present-day town development. In the sixties a comprehensive plan for town development and housing was drawn up, in accordance with which new large housing estates, new public buildings and new highways were built, and the old districts of the city were reconstructed. A separate plan provides for the unearthing and reconstruction of historical monuments. The Royal Palace of Buda has been rebuilt and now serves cultural purposes; excavations have brought to light remains of the old palaces in the site. Parallel to the large-scale constructions, the east-west and the north-south line of the Metro have been completed. At the same time the pattern of traffic in the streets is being accordingly changed. New, modern hotels have been built and more are under construction; everything is changing; the city improves and develops from day to day.

Finding One's Way in Budapest

Our book presents the most important sights of the capital arranged in several "walks" so that even those who stay in Budapest for only a short time may acquaint themselves with the city's main sights, and with its life and atmosphere. The Castle District, so rich in historic and art monuments, Óbuda, Aquincum, the Inner City, the Danube bank and the City Park are among the first places that should be visited.

The regular plan on which the town is built makes orientation easy. The Danube, flowing from north to south, divides Budapest into two approximately equal parts, and the boulevards form semicircles running from one bridge to another. One branch of the boulevard in Buda leads from Margaret Bridge to Elizabeth Bridge, the other goes farther south to Petőfi Bridge. In Pest the "Little Boulevard" (Kiskörút) runs from the Chain Bridge to Liberty Bridge, the "Great Boulevard" (Nagykörút) from Margaret Bridge to Petőfi Bridge, and the outer boulevard from Árpád Bridge to the Southern Railway Bridge; the boulevards are intersected by radial highways.

Recommended Walks

(Numbers in brackets refer to chapters containing detailed information)

ONE-DAY PROGRAMME

In the morning: the Castle District (1), the Palace (2)
In the afternoon: the Inner City (3), the Parliament building and its neighbourhood (4)

TWO-DAY PROGRAMME

The first day
In the morning: Gellért Hill (5), the Inner City (3), the Parliament building and its neighbourhood (4)
In the afternoon: the Castle District (1), the Palace (2)

The second day
In the morning: the Buda Danube bank, the Király, Lukács and Császár baths, Óbuda, Aquincum (6), Margaret Island (7)
In the afternoon: Hősök tere (Heroes' Square), the Museum of Fine Arts (8), the City Park (9)

THREE-DAY PROGRAMME

The first day
In the morning: the Inner City (3), the Parliament building and its neighbourhood (4), the Ethnographical Museum (15)
In the afternoon: the Castle District (1), the Palace and its museums (2)

The second day
In the morning: Gellért Hill, Tabán (5), the Buda Danube bank and Water Town, Aquincum (6)
In the afternoon: Szent István körút, the Basilica, Népköztársaság útja (10), Hősök tere, the Museum of Fine Arts (8), the City Park (9), the Zoo (13)

The third day
In the morning: the National Museum and the Museum of Applied Arts (11), Margaret Island (7)
In the afternoon: excursion to the Buda hills (12) or in summer, a trip by pleasure-boat on the Danube

FOUR-DAY PROGRAMME

The first, second and third days
As in the three-day programme

On the fourth day
You will no doubt choose a walk to suit your taste:
For lovers of nature: the Buda hills (12), Margaret Island (7), the Zoo (13)
If you are interested in the subterranean world: the caves (14)
If you are interested in the history of architecture: historical monuments (15)
For those who like fine arts and ethnography (16)
Budapest for music-lovers (17)
Budapest, the city of baths (18)
For sports lovers (19)
Places of technological interest (20)

FIVE-DAY PROGRAMME

The first, second, third and fourth days
As in the four-day programme

The fifth day
Excursion to the Danube Bend (21)

Walks

1

THE CASTLE DISTRICT

The Castle District in Buda is the ancient kernel of the capital's right-bank settlement. Everything that surrounds it was once only suburbs. From whatever direction you reach the Castle District, you cross the ramparts which completely encircle Castle Hill. The whole area within the ramparts is protected as an ancient monument: the lines of the streets and the foundations and architectural remains of the buildings retain the atmosphere and memories of the medieval and eighteenth and nineteenth-century capital.

Approach: As Castle Hill rises 50 to 60 metres (165 to 200 ft.) above the Danube, the inhabitants of Budapest rightly say that they go "up" to the Castle. The serpentine road, from which there is a magnificent view, starts out from the Buda end of the Chain Bridge. Motorists are banned from the Castle District, and only those possessing special permits are allowed in. It is therefore advisable to leave the car at one of the large parking places. Buses 16 and 116 follow the winding road up to the Castle District. The other main route to the Castle District starts from Moszkva tér, the traffic centre of Northern Buda, and reaches Castle Hill via the Vienna Gate (Bécsi kapu). You can also get to the Royal Castle by a funicular railway from the Chain Bridge, or directly by lift from Dózsa György tér. However, the pleasantest approach is on foot. You can start from any of the main streets running round the hill—Fő utca, Batthyány utca or Attila utca—and by taking the quiet little streets, steps or slopes cut in the castle walls, you reach the Castle District in a very few minutes.

The Royal Palace as seen from the Danube Promenade in Pest

A little history. The building of the town began in the middle of the thirteenth century. At the time of the 1241 Mongol invasion the town of Pest, built on the plain on the site of today's Inner City and thus completely defenceless, had been burnt down and its population put to the sword. Thus it seemed safer to build a new city protected by ramparts on the other side of the river, on the plateau on top of the steep limestone hill. The Royal Castle was built at the southern end of the plateau, the civilian town to the north. At first the town was protected only by fences and the walls of the houses, but by the early sixteenth century it was surrounded by strong ramparts. This is why the Turks in 1541 did not lay siege to Buda but captured it by trickery; later they further fortified the ramparts. It was only after repeated sieges that the united Christian armies succeeded in 1686 in recapturing Buda Castle. The country then came under the rule of the Habsburg Emperor Leopold. The city of Buda was almost completely destroyed by the siege and only a handful of inhabitants remained; therefore, in order to repopulate the town, settlers were invited from abroad. The former capital sank to the status of a small provincial town in the Habsburg Empire. Then, during the eighteenth century, a little Baroque town grew up on the medieval ruins. Not much more than 150 years after the Turkish devastations, in 1849, during the Hungarian War of Independence, the Castle was again besieged and it was only in 1867—when, as a result of the Compromise with the Habsburg dynasty, an independent

A street in the Castle District—as it was destroyed in the Second World War

Hungarian government was created—that the Castle District once more became the administrative centre of the country. Towards the end of the Second World War, it was in the Castle District that the last Nazi German troops concentrated and held out, from the end of December 1944 until the middle of February 1945, when the Soviet Red Army liberated the capital after a siege lasting almost two months. As a consequence of the Germans' bitter resistance the Castle District again suffered enormous damage. Part of the medieval remains that can now be seen were discovered during the reconstruction of houses which were found to have been built upon the foundations of earlier ones.

The **Fishermen's Bastion** is one of the most popular spots of the Castle District with visitors, as it offers a grand panorama of almost the entire city. It is situated at the eastern side of Castle Hill, and can be reached from the centre of the district, Szentháromság tér (Trinity Square). Its architecture is characteristic of the turn of the century; its flights of stairs, its projections, its turrets, and its ambulatory-like galleries make it a mixture of the neo-Gothic and neo-Romanesque styles and of the romantic baronial castles. In 1901–3, the aim of its architect, Frigyes Schulek, was to provide a worthy setting for the Church of Our Lady (Matthias Church); when building it he also made use of the remaining stones of the old Castle wall. The Fishermen's Bastion received its name from the medieval ramparts system which rose above the suburb named Fishermen's Town; furthermore, there used to be a fish-market behind the ramparts. Beneath the Fishermen's Bastion lies the old suburb of Víziváros (Water Town), now full of new buildings; its Baroque church towers recall the past. Looking towards the north we get a view of the Danube with Margaret Island. The building which dominates the panorama of the Pest bank is that of the *Parliament* with its dome and spires. At the head of the Chain Bridge in Pest, facing the *Hotel Forum* and the *Hotel Atrium Hyatt* stands the building of the *Hungarian Academy of Sciences,* with the dome of the *Basilica* in the background. Further down the block of the *Hotel Duna Inter-Continental* becomes visible. The church towers between the Chain Bridge and Elizabeth Bridge are reminders of the past of the Inner City of Pest. Beyond the vast, sombre mass of the buildings of Pest, there rise in a semicircle the high-rise blocks of the new housing estates built in the 1960s. Casting our glance

The Fishermen's Bastion

towards the south we see the *Chain Bridge* (Lánchíd), built in 1849 in neo-Classical style, rebuilt in 1949; further to the south the most recently reconstructed bridge, *Elizabeth Bridge* (Erzsébet-híd)—inaugurated in 1964—spans the river. The panorama ends at the dolomite rocks of Gellért Hill.

Below Fishermen's Bastion, in a bend of the road, stands the *statue of János Hunyadi* (the work of István Tóth). János Hunyadi—the future King Matthias' father—was a famous military commander who in 1456 repulsed the Turkish attack at Nándorfehérvár (today's Belgrade); it was to commemorate his victory that Pope Calixtus III ordered that church bells should be sounded every noon. Not far away stands a replica of the famous *statue of Saint George,* by the Kolozsvári brothers. (The 1373 original can be seen in Prague.) In the upper court of the Fishermen's Bastion stands an *equestrian statue of (Saint) Stephen I* (by Alajos Stróbl, 1906), the first king of Hungary (1001–1038) and founder of the State.

The **Church of Our Lady** is generally called the *Matthias Church,* because its southern tower bears the coat of arms with the raven (in Latin: *Corvus*) of Matthias (Corvinus) Hunyadi (1458–1490). In the thirteenth century Buda's first parish church stood here. In the fourteenth century it was rebuilt as a Gothic hall church, but its construction, just as that of so many Gothic churches in Europe, was never finished, and the northern tower was not built. In Turkish times it became the main mosque and its interior furnishings were destroyed.

During the 1686 siege its tower and roof collapsed. Later on the church was rebuilt in the Baroque style, and in the last decades of the nineteenth century Frigyes Schulek (1841–1919) reconstructed, from the excavated medieval remains, the original Gothic church, the one in which Charles Robert (1308–1342) and Sigismund of Luxembourg (1387–1437) had been crowned, and in which the wedding of King Matthias with Catherine Podebrad in 1463 and with Beatrice of Aragon in 1470 had been solemnized. The last two kings of Hungary, Francis Joseph I and Charles IV, were also crowned in this church, in 1867 and 1916 respectively. During the Second World War the damage suffered by the church was so heavy that it took two decades to repair it.

From outside the most beautiful part of the church is the 80-metre (260 ft.) high stone-laced Gothic tower. The southern portal is decorated by a fourteenth-century relief depicting Virgin Mary's death. Inside, the plastered walls are painted with coloured ornamental design. The frescoes depict the lives of Hungarian saints. In the northern part there is a series of chapels; in the one nearest to the chancel the sarcophagi of Béla III (1173–1196) and his wife Anne of Châtillon can be seen; they were brought here from Székesfehérvár.

Near the chancel, in the former crypt, we find a museum of stonework remains, including medieval carvings. In the gallery a *collection of ecclesiastical art* is exhibited, containing old chalices and vestments as well as a replica of the crown of the Hungarian kings.

Szentháromság tér (Trinity Square) and its neighbourhood. In the Middle Ages the Church of Our

The Church of Our Lady as seen from the Parliament

Lady—just like other churches built in towns surrounded by walls—was wedged in a narrow street and rose above the surrounding low houses. It was only in the Baroque period that Szentháromság tér was laid out and it became the centre of the district. Opposite the church is the former *Town Hall* of Buda which now houses a research institute of the Academy of Sciences (2 Szentháromság utca); its ridge-turret recalls the former chapel. On the corner of the building stands the statue of Pallas Athene, the patron of the town, holding the coat of arms of Buda. The Baroque *Trinity Statue* in the centre of the square was erected by the citizens in the eighteenth century in thanksgiving for their escape from the plague. In 1925–30 it was almost completely re-carved; the damage caused by the Second World War was repaired in 1968. To the north of the statue, the neo-Gothic building, built in the spirit of eclecticism, is the former *Ministry of Finance,* which now houses the newly-established Central Hungarian Archives. The short *Szentháromság utca* starts opposite Matthias Church. In the barrel-vaulted doorways of *Nos.* 5 and 7 medieval doors and Gothic niches with seats have been found, the latter a rarity in dwelling-houses. In *No.* 7 the Ruszwurm pastry-shop, opened in 1827, still functions, with its original furnishings.

The little street leads to the western end of Castle Hill, the **Tóth Árpád Promenade**. The view we saw from the Fishermen's Bastion can now be complemented by the panorama which unfolds from here. Below in the valley lie the inner districts of Buda. The huge park in the centre is the Vérmező (Blood Meadow); further on the modern buildings of the Southern Railway Station and the *Hotel Buda Penta* can be seen. The view extends as far as the Buda hills. To the northwest their highest point is the 529 metre (1750 ft.) János Hill, with a look-out tower on top. Not far from it the Television Tower is visible; on the south side the last of the hills is the Gellért Hill. A hundred years ago the slopes of the hills below the woods were covered with vines; Buda wines were famous. In the 1870s phylloxera destroyed the vineyards, which have now been replaced by garden suburbs. The promenade itself dates back to Turkish times; below it runs the so-called Long Wall of the Castle District's western ramparts. It was fortified with several round bastions, the largest of which, at the northern end of the *War History Museum,* is the so-called Esztergom Bastion. The can-

The Castle District: the Church of Our Lady

nons, made in Hungarian and foreign foundries and used in defence of or against the walls of Buda, are also exhibited here.

From the Tóth Árpád Promenade we return to Szentháromság tér. **Hess András tér** adjoins Szentháromság tér to north. This little square bears all the characteristics of the Castle District. On its eastern side, near the Church of Our Lady, stands the Budapest Hilton hotel. The southern façade of the modern building completed in 1976 has preserved the Baroque and Louis XVI style of an old school building dating from the end of the eighteenth century. In the axis of the hotel stands the base of a tower decorated with magnificent curtain-arched windows, above which once rose the tower of the Dominican monastery, built in the thirteenth–fifteenth centuries. In the western wall there is a copy of the King Matthias statue of Bautzen. In the open courtyard of the southern wing the groundwalls of the one-time monastery can be seen. From the bastion a view opens into the aisle of the one-time chapel, which is the scene of open-air musical performances in summer. The house at *No. 3 Hess András tér* was rebuilt in the early eighteenth century on thirteenth-century foundations; in 1760 it housed the *Red Hedgehog* (Vörös Sün) *Inn,* as can still be seen on the carved stone inn-sign above the gate. It was here that in the eighteenth century the first theatrical performances in Buda were held. The house at *No. 4.* facing the hotel was formed by joining together the remains of three fourteenth-century houses. The first book printed in Hungary, the *Chronica Hungarorum,* was produced here in 1473 by the printer András Hess. Behind the neo-Classical exteriors of the house, richly decorated Gothic niches with seats, doorframes and barrel-vaulted halls were revealed after the Second World War. Today it houses the *Fortuna restaurant,* a visitor to which finds himself in authentic medieval surroundings. In the centre of the square stands a statue of *Pope Innocent XI,* erected in memory of the pontiff's appeal in 1686 for a Christian league to liberate Buda.

Further walks in the Castle District. From the centre of Castle Hill four parallel streets run due north, and two due south, all of which can be explored in an hour's or an hour and a half's walk. If you have time, we recommend you to walk along one of them to Bécsikapu tér, to come back along another one, have a little rest on the Tóth Árpád Promenade or in one of the old-fashioned pastry-shops or restaurants, and then to continue your walk, admiring the lovely old buildings and remembering to look into their doorways and inner courts. The streets of the district are sometimes broken by bends or slopes, and therefore you can often only see parts of them at a time. Owing to the influence of Italian architecture, the tops of the houses run parallel to the

The Castle District: a section of the Tóth Árpád Promenade

axis of the streets, which results in a restful and harmonious picture. It is this juxtaposition of historically interesting buildings that gives the district its pleasant atmosphere of the past. Even on newer façades, we often find medieval door and windowframes, frescoes or upper floors projecting on arches, and niches with seats in the doorways. No explanation has as yet been offered for this last feature of the architecture of medieval Buda. It is assumed that the servants of guests visiting the noblemen and rich citizens used to wait in these niches for their masters; in fact, those wishing to taste the wine of the house were probably also served here.

The Castle District with the Lutheran Church

It is perhaps in *Táncsics Mihály utca* that the most beautiful Baroque dwelling-houses and palaces can be found. The Baroque mansion at *No. 7*—which was also built from several medieval houses—witnessed in 1800 a visit by Ludwig van Beethoven and today houses the Institute for Musicology of the Hungarian Academy of Sciences and the Museum of Musical History. *No. 9*, which now presents neo-Classical features, was used in medieval times to be the Royal Mint. In the nineteenth century several champions of the Hungarian independence movement were imprisoned in the street wing (the barracks), built around 1810. In *No. 26* archaeologists have recently excavated the remains of the synagogue of the medieval Jewish community. The *Vienna Gate* (Bécsi kapu) is the only existing old towngate of Buda; it has been rebuilt in neo-Classical style. A memorial plaque in Latin (1936) is dedicated to the international Christian army which in 1686 recaptured the town from the Turks. On Bécsi kapu tér the late Baroque *dwelling-houses* at *Nos. 5–8* form a pleasant and often photographed complex of monuments. In 1935–37 Thomas Mann stayed several times in *No. 7* as a guest of Baron Lajos Hatvany, the eminent patron of letters. At the northern end of the square rises the huge block of the Hungarian National Archives. On *Kapisztrán tér* stands the solitary tower of the *Mary Magdalene Church*. This used to be the town's second parish church and is mentioned in a document dating from 1276. During the Turkish occupation it was the only Christian church in Buda and was used both by Protes-

The Castle District: Bécsi kapu tér (Vienna Gate Square)

The Castle District: a dwelling-house in Országház utca

tants and Catholics. Its nave and chancel were destroyed in the Second World War.

The Golden Age of Buda, the fifteenth century, is best illustrated by the buildings at *Nos. 18–22* in *Országház utca*. Many similar Gothic buildings lined the streets at that time. Proceeding southwards from Szentháromság tér, *Nos. 14–16* in *Tárnok utca* offer a similar sight. An attentive visitor walking along *Úri utca, Fortuna utca* and *Dísz tér* will discover many other beautiful things, medieval, Baroque and neo-Classical mansions. Gothic details can also be discerned behind the more recent exteriors, since newly discovered remains have been built into the buildings during their reconstruction.

Reconstructed in 1978, the Castle Theatre stands in *Színház utca,* which comes off Dísz tér. Originally housing a Carmelite convent, this Louis XVI building was converted into a theatre in the eighteenth century by Farkas Kempelen, the inventor of the chess machine and the talking machine.

2

THE ROYAL PALACE AND ITS MUSEUMS

Owing to the construction work still going on, the former Royal Palace, which houses valuable collections, is at present best reached either on foot from Szarvas tér near Elizabeth Bridge from the north, from Dísz tér situated on the edge of Castle District, by funicular railway departing from the Buda end of the Chain Bridge from the east, and by lift from Dózsa György tér from the west.

A little history. The construction of the Royal Palace was begun in the middle of the thirteenth century, and was continued in the fourteenth century by King Louis the Great who had a keep built here. The building of the outer walls and of the western fortifications was not finished until the end of the century. In the fifteenth century Sigismund of Luxembourg continued the construction and added a chapel and a palace. Construction work reached its peak with King Matthias, who had the southeastern fortifications built, as well as a Renaissance Royal Palace. In the late fifteenth century the King of Hungary's palace was one of the most splendid royal seats in Europe. His famous library, the Bibliotheca Corviniana, according to his contemporaries, equalled the Medici Library in Florence. During Turkish times the palace became increasingly neglected and was finally destroyed in the great siege of 1686. In 1715 the medieval ruins were cleared. The building of the southern wing of the present-day palace was started in the eighteenth century during the reign of Maria Theresa, first to the plans of the chief court architect J. N. Jadot and later according to the designs of F. A. Hillebrandt and Ignác Oracsek. The other parts were built at the end of the nineteenth century, during the

The Royal Palace: part of the Castle Museum

The Royal Palace: the southern fortifications

reign of Francis Joseph I, to the plans of Alajos Hauszman (1847–1926) and Miklós Ybl (1814–1891). (From 1790 the Palatine representing the Habsburg kings lived in the palaces.) In March 1800 Joseph Haydn conducted in it his oratorio *The Creation*. In the siege of 1944–45 the palace collapsed and was burnt down. During its rebuilding the remains of the medieval palaces and fortifications were excavated. When completely reconstructed and repaired, the entire complex of buildings will serve cultural purposes.

Visiting the *Palace* should begin with a look its exterior. The main façade overlooking the Danube is 304 metres (334 yds.) long, with columns arranged symmetrically, in Baroque style on both sides of the dome. In front of the central part of the building there is a statue of Prince Eugene of Savoy who was one of the leaders of the armies that liberated Buda Castle in 1686. The statue at the gate of the palace garden represents the *Turul,* the mythic bird of the ancient Magyars. The neo-Baroque groups of buildings towards the south and north are simpler in style. *The fortifications* of the palace date from the Middle Ages. To the south, facing Gellért Hill, the large *Round Bastion,* 40 metres (44 yds.) in diameter, and the *Gate Tower* with its tent roof, dominate the scene. In front of the Round Bastion on the slope of the hill a group of excavated Turkish tombstones presents an interesting sight. Passing through the Baroque gate cut in the outer wall we reach the walls and passages of the fortifications.

The palace has two inner courts, an open and a closed one. In the open court there is a fountain with a group of statues, the most interesting of which is that of King Matthias in the hunting gear of the age.

The entrances to two museums are in this court. One leads to the *Hungarian National Gallery* (see p. 110) in the centre of the complex, whereas the *Museum of the Hungarian Working-Class Movement* is housed in the wing to the north. The southern wing contains the Castle *Museum* (the Budapest History Museum) which displays the history of the Palace and the city, the Gothic halls and the recently excavated Gothic sculptures. Its halls house exhibitions from Budapest's history as well as other periodical exhibitions. From the windows facing the Danube we can see the Inner City, one-time Pest, just as the Palace's inhabitants did in the nineteenth century. The building complex located on the western side of the Lion's Courtyard now houses the *National Széchényi Library*.

3

THE INNER CITY

Up to the first third of the eighteenth century the left-bank settlement, the historic centre of the former town of Pest, consisted only of the district lying between today's Liberty Bridge, Chain Bridge, Múzeum körút and Tanács körút, that is to say, it extended only as far as today's Kis-körút (Little Boulevard). The town was completely rebuilt and it grew gradually; today, of the original town of Pest, there only remain some parts of the fifteenth-century town walls, and from the eighteenth century, only the churches, as well as a few monasteries and public buildings. In contrast to the Castle District of Buda, which is by-passed by the main traffic of the city, the Inner City, with its shops, offices and important traffic arteries, is part of the city's everyday life.

A little history. On the site of today's Inner City Parish Church, in the so-called "Barbarians' land", a strong watchtower was erected in 294 A.D. by the Romans; this they called Contra-Aquincum. At the time of the Magyar Conquest, around 900, the tower was used for defence and around it was built a town which, however, was completely destroyed by the Mongol invasion of 1241. The new town was built on the Castle Hill in Buda, and Pest remained a kind of suburb, though owing to the Diets being held in the Field of Rákos, in the outskirts of the town, and to the national fairs held in Pest, traffic and commercial life remained busy. In the late fifteenth century Pest was surrounded by walls, the site of which is revealed by the remains of some buildings originally built against them: some stones of the walls and of the town gates can still be seen. In 1541 Pest was captured by the Turks, together with Buda, and its social and economic life declined during the 150 years of occupation. After its liberation, in the early eighteenth century, it received independent city rights and its development was greatly furthered by the rebirth of commerce. In 1785 the Hungarian University of Nagyszombat (now Trnava, Czechoslovakia) moved to Pest, and thanks to this, the city became in the next decade the centre of the country's intellectual life. However, in 1838 the great Danube flood swept away almost all the old houses. Once reconstructed, the town began to develop by leaps and bounds, leaving Buda far behind. At the turn of the century, when the old Elizabeth Bridge was built, the new buildings along the main roads gave Pest a characteristic eclectic character.

The Roosevelt tér (the Pest end of the Chain Bridge) and its neighbourhood. "Hungary is not dead; she will live again!"—this is how, in the first part of the nineteenth century, Count István Széchenyi, one of the greatest figures of the Reform Period, whom Lajos Kossuth called "the greatest Hungarian", encouraged the nation, groaning under foreign oppression. He himself whole-heartedly urged and sponsored the building of factories, mills, roads and bridges. It was on his initiative, and according to his ideas, that the *Chain Bridge* was built from 1839 to 1849 to the plans of the English engineer *William Tierney Clark* by *Adam Clark,* a Scot. The bridge, 380 metres (420 yds.) long and 15.7 metres (17.5 yds.) wide, is supported by pillars shaped like antique triumphal arches. It was the first bridge over the Danube and it not only linked Buda with Pest but also the western with the eastern parts of the country. In January 1945 Hitler's troops blew it up, but in 1948–49 it was rebuilt in its original form.

From the Pest end of the bridge the panorama of Buda unfolds before us. Towards the north the view extends to the Buda hills and to Margaret Bridge on the Danube. On Castle Hill the graceful spire of the Church of Our Lady rises high above us, with the Hotel Hilton to the north and the turrets and terraces of the Fishermen's Bastion in front, and the remains of the old castle walls below it. Baroque church towers rise above the great mass of houses of Water Town. Opposite us stands the Royal Palace, with its medieval fortifications. To the south we see the rocky *Gellért Hill* with the *Citadel* and the *Liberation Monument* on top. The newest bridge over the Danube, Elizabeth Bridge, inaugurated in 1903 and reconstructed in 1964, is 380 metres (420 yds.) long and 27.5 metres (30.5 yds.) wide. Further down we see *Liberty Bridge* and, in the distance, *Petőfi Bridge.*

Two statues stand in the centre of Roosevelt tér; the standing figure represents Count István Széchenyi, the sitting one Ferenc Deák, one of the great figures of nineteenth-century Hungarian liberalism. To the north the square is closed in by the neo-Renaissance palace of the *Hungarian Academy of Sciences,* built in 1862–64, founded in 1830 on the initiative of István Széchenyi. Parallel with the Danube, the *Hotel Forum* stands on

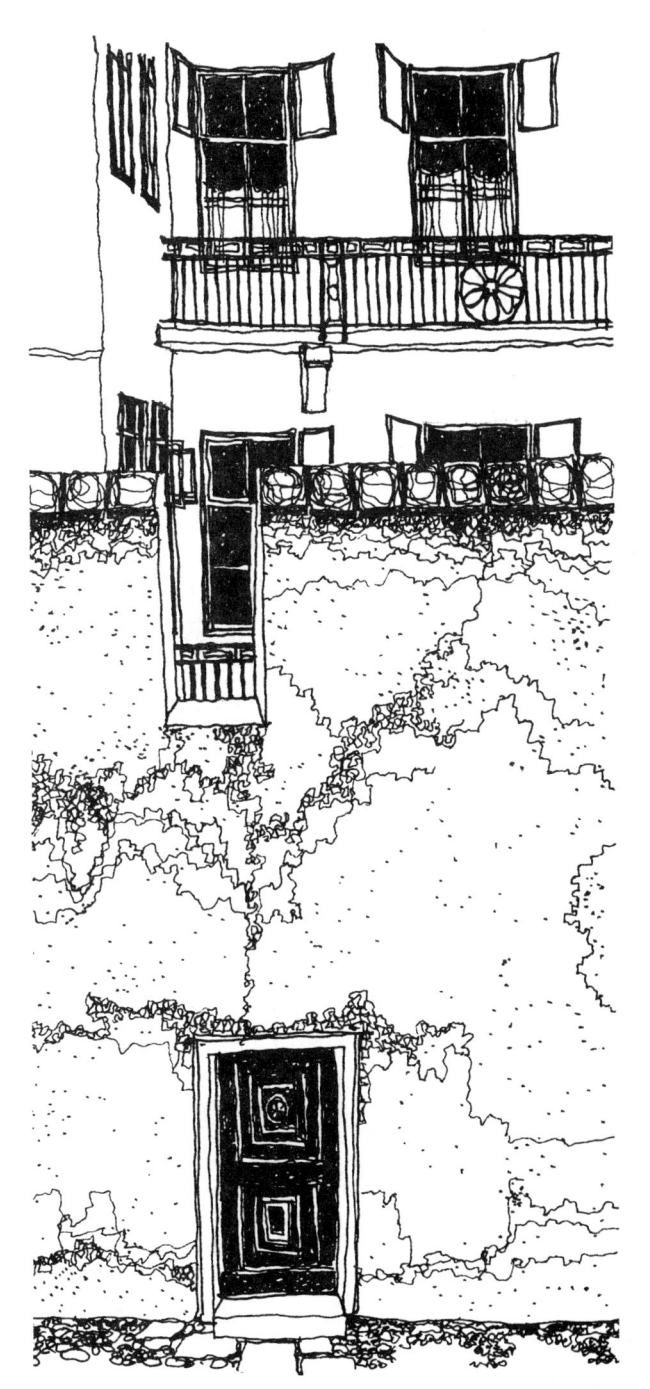

Remains of the old town wall of Pest in Magyar utca

Elizabeth Bridge and the oldest part of the Inner City

the southern side of the square, with the *Hotel Atrium Hyatt* behind it. From Roosevelt tér Dorottya utca leads us to Vörösmarty tér.

Vörösmarty tér, Váci utca. The square (Vörösmarty tér) is one of the busiest centres of the Inner City. Here are the air terminals and the offices of most foreign airline companies. Many bus-routes go near the square and the old underground railway has its terminal here. In the centre of the square is a statue of Mihály Vörösmarty, the great Hungarian poet of the nineteenth century. A glance round the square reveals a big fashion store, several travel offices, some antique shops and an old pastry-shop, the *Gerbeaud*, which was originally founded by the famous Swiss confectioner. Not only the furnishings and atmosphere of the pastry-shop preserve its old traditions but also the quality of its products. A new building rises on the Danube side of the square: this "palace of culture" houses several musical establishments, publishing houses and editorial offices; on the ground-floor are a record shop, an exhibition hall and a concert agency and on the first floor we find a concert hall. It is adjoined on the Danube side by a Romantic-style building, the *Vigadó* (Concert Hall), built in 1859–64 to the designs of Frigyes Feszl (1821–1884); this is an early and important manifesta-

The Chain Bridge

tion of Hungarian Romantic architecture; it played a significant part in the social and artistic life of the capital, and was the scene of great balls and receptions. The most famous artists of the world performed in the concert hall. Since its reconstruction in 1980, it is once more the scene of popular concerts. The façade is decorated with symbolic figures connected with music and dance and with statues of the great men of Hungarian history. The obelisk in the little square in front of the Vigadó was erected to the memory of the Soviet soldiers who died fighting for the liberation of the capital.

To the south of Vörösmarty tér starts Váci utca, which, together with the neighbouring streets, is the chief shopping centre of Budapest, with many gift and fashion shops. It also contains some interesting buildings. For instance, *No. 9* used to be an inn (it was rebuilt in 1840 by József Hild), in the banquet-hall of which the 11-year-old Ferenc Liszt once gave a concert. Today it houses the Pest Theatre. The façade of *No. 11* is covered with Zsolnay ceramics. The house at *No. 20* houses the *Hotel Taverna,* and facing it is the International Commercial Centre; both were built in 1985. Kristóf tér leads to *Martinelli tér* where the Art Nouveau ornaments on the house at *No. 5* strike the eye, and further, behind the Baroque façade of the *Servite Church,* we can see the beautiful Baroque building of the *Town Hall* (9–11 Városház utca, V). It was built between 1727 and 1735 to the designs of the Italian architect Martinelli to house disabled ex-service men. Since 1894 it has been the Central Municipal Town Hall. The 190 metre (210 yds.) long façade with its 47 windows, surmounted in the centre by the tower of the former chapel, is an impressive sight. The neo-Classical building at *No. 7 Városház utca,* now the Pest County Hall, was also built in the first part of the nineteenth century. In its artistically designed courtyard open-air concerts are held.

The Inner City Parish Church and the Pest end of Elizabeth Bridge. Over the wall of the one-time Roman *castrum* a chapel was built which was later extended into a Romanesque basilica and, in the fifteenth century, into a Gothic hall church. In Turkish times the church suffered much damage—the choir was used as a mosque. A relic of this is a unique Muslim prayer-niche or *mihrab,* which has been preserved in the wall of the chancel facing Mecca, towards the southeast. The church received its present Baroque form between

Váci utca

1725 and 1775. In 1933 it was again renovated and the Gothic parts were restored. Of its two towers one was destroyed during the war; it has now been rebuilt. The external walls, with the Gothic flying buttresses and carved doors, are also evidence of the building's past. Inside, the most magnificent sight is the choir, with 19 Gothic sedilia and remains of frescoes from the beginning of the fifteenth century. There is a row of chapels on both sides of the nave. In the chapels nearest to the choir carved Renaissance tabernacle niches were built in the walls at the beginning of the sixteenth century.

Budapest Town Hall

Pest County Hall

On the main altar and in the baptistry the works of contemporary Hungarian artists are in harmony with the different artistic styles. To the north of the church the *Garden of Ruins* displays an excavated corner-tower of the Roman fortress Contra-Aquincum and the adjoining foundation walls, while notice-boards show the layout of the fortress system excavated in the environs of the capital. The modern group of statues on the fountain represents Roman legionaries in battle.

The Danube bank is only a few steps from the church. *Elizabeth Bridge,* suspended on pylons on the two banks, was rebuilt in 1964. North of it, on the riverside promenade, rises the modern building of the Hotel Duna Inter-Continental, completed in 1970. Next to it on the little square we see the statue of Sándor Petőfi

The choir of the Inner City Parish Church

(1823–1849), who brought a new, deeply lyrical, yet popular spirit to Hungarian poetry; he was the immortal poet of the 1848–49 Revolution and War of Independence and he died on the battlefield fighting for Hungary's freedom.

The little Baroque mansion at *No. 2 Pesti Barnabás utca* (off Petőfi tér), which now houses the *Százéves*

(Hundred-year-old) *restaurant*, is the only example of eighteenth-century secular Baroque architecture in Pest. It was built in 1755 by András Mayerhoffer; the restaurant was opened in 1831.

Further walks in the Inner City. The line formed by Szabadsajtó út—Kossuth Lajos utca—Rákóczi út, starting from Elizabeth Bridge, is the chief commercial artery of Pest; it divides the Inner City into two parts. A few steps from the bridge, on *Felszabadulás tér*, stands the old *Franciscan Church*. In the early Middle Ages here was the city boundary. The present Baroque church was constructed between 1727 and 1743, on the foundations of an earlier church which itself had been rebuilt from a Turkish mosque. The tower of the church

The Little Boulevard with the Basilica and the Lutheran Church

stands, as is usual with the Franciscans, at the back, next to the chancel, with a neo-Gothic spire. On the Kossuth Lajos utca side of the church there is a relief by Barnabás Holló (1905) in honour of Miklós Wesselényi, who saved many lives during the great 1838 flood. Passing the façade of the church we reach *Károlyi Mihály utca.* The neo-Renaissance building at *No. 10* houses the University Library; the frescoes in the reading room were painted by Károly Lotz. The precious collection of books includes, among others, eleven Corvinae. *No. 16,* the former palace of the Károlyi family, is now the *Petőfi Literary Museum.* A point of historical interest about the building is that here, in the autumn of 1849, the Austrian commander-in-chief Haynau, who took revenge for the 1848–49 Hungarian War of Independence, signed the death sentence of many Hungarian *honvéd* (national army) officers and politicians of the independence movement. A memorial plaque is dedicated to the last private owner of the palace, *Mihály* (Michael) *Károlyi,* the President of the 1918 Hungarian Republic. On *Egyetem tér* (University Square) stands the central building of the *Eötvös Loránd University of Sciences.* Next to the university building stands the most beautiful Baroque ecclesiastical monument in the capital, the *University Church.* It was built for the Paulite friars between 1725 and 1742. The towers are topped by the bulb-shaped spires so characteristic of Pest and Buda churches. The oak gate, framed by columns, half-columns and stone carvings, is especially remarkable. All the furnishings and ornaments in the interior of the church, the carvings on the benches as well as the group of statues on the pulpit, date from the time it was built.

The Inner City is encircled by the so-called *Little Boulevard* running along the line of the former city walls from Deák tér through Tanács körút, Múzeum körút, Tolbuhin körút and Dimitrov tér to Liberty Bridge. This busy thoroughfare used to be the starting-point of country roads; today wide avenues opening from it will take you to the main national highways. The most beautiful building on the Little Boulevard is the *National Museum* (14–16 Múzeum körút; see p. 88). In front of the façade, in the garden stands the *statue of János Arany* (by Alajos Stróbl, 1893), the great Hungar-

"The Paris Arcade" (the passage leading from Felszabadulás tér to Petőfi Sándor utca)

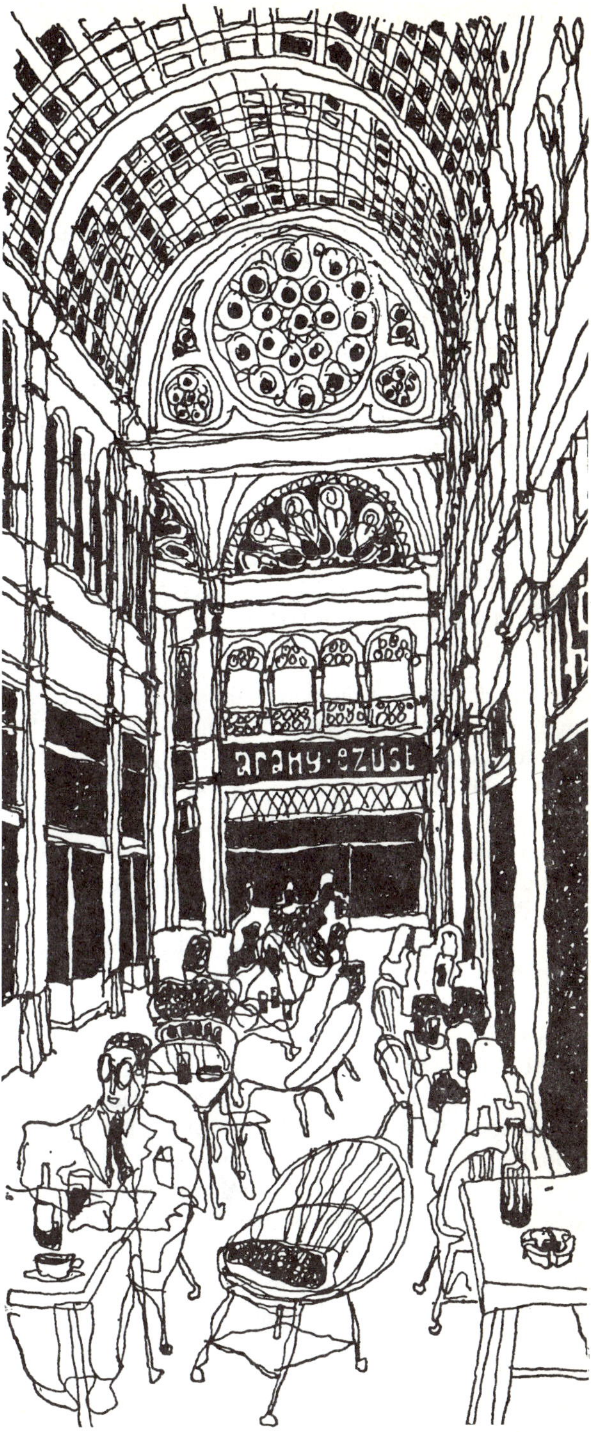
arany·ezüst

ian epic poet of the nineteenth century. Majestic neo-Classical harmony characterizes the museum, which was built between 1837 and 1847 to the designs of Mihály Pollack (1773–1855). To the north of the busy street, beyond Rákóczi út, at the corner of Tanács körút and Dohány utca, it is worth stopping to look at the striking *Synagogue,* topped by bulb-shaped towers, which was built in 1854–59 in Romantic Byzantine-Moorish style. An interesting building in Deák tér is the neo-Classical *Lutheran Church.* In Deák tér the Little Boulevard forks: one branch, Bajcsy-Zsilinszky út, leads to Szent István körút, the other, József Attila utca, passing by a Metro station where the three lines meet and the Engels tér bus terminal, closes the semicircle leading to the Danube.

4

THE PARLIAMENT BUILDING AND ITS NEIGHBOURHOOD

This district, built at the end of the nineteenth century on the site of timber-depots, mills and barracks, is a few minutes' walk from the Chain Bridge (along the Danube embankment), from the Inner City (through the streets leading northwards), or from the Margaret Bridge. The most beautiful eclectic and pseudo-historical public buildings were erected in this district. The high dome of the Parliament building guides pedestrians and motorists alike. Among city transport services there are tramways, trolleybuses and a Metro station at *Kossuth Lajos tér,* the 6,500 sq.m. (about 7,800 sq.yds.) square in front of the Parliament building.

The Parliament building, which has become the symbol of the capital, was built between 1880 and 1902 to the designs of Imre Steindl. The alluvial soil of the Danube bank had to be reinforced by a two-metre (7 ft.) deep concrete foundation so that it support the colossal building, which is 268 metres (300 yds.) long and 123 metres (140 yds.) at its greatest width, has ten courts, 27 gates, and 29 staircases. The exterior of the building is adorned with lace-like Gothic pinnacles and 88 statues representing Hungarian rulers, princes and military commanders. On the Danube side an unbroken line of arcades dominates the building, with neo-Gothic and neo-Renaissance motifs. In the centre

The Parliament building as seen from Castle Hill

of the building, in Kossuth Lajos tér, is the main entrance, flanked by bronze lions, behind which the ornamental staircase leads to the hall under the dome.

Guided tours are organized to see the interior. The 27-metre (82 ft.) high hall beneath the dome—which in 1896 saw the session of Parliament in honour of the millennium of the Conquest of the country and where today state awards are presented—is decorated all round with the coats of arms of the former Hungarian counties. On the heads of the sixteen clustered pillars the statues of Hungarian rulers can be seen. The interior of the building has been symmetrically arranged, because the Hungarian parliament was originally composed of two houses: the rooms were built around the assembly halls of the Upper and Lower Houses—now the Congress Hall and the Assembly Hall respectively—with the Delegation Hall in the centre. Some interesting ornaments of the lobbies are the painted pyrogranite statues. The frescoes, paintings and tapestries—the works of Mihály Munkácsy, Károly Lotz and Gyula Rudnay, among others—depict scenes from Hungarian history and legends.

The offices of the Presidential Council of the People's Republic and of the Council of Ministers, as well as the Parliament Library, are also to be found in the Parliament building. In the hall under the dome a Christmas tree is set up every year for schoolchildren, the pioneers.

The two other large buildings in Kossuth Lajos tér are the eclectic building of the Ethnographical Museum (see p. 112) and the Ministry of Agriculture and Food. A newly erected modern building on the square houses the Chamber of Economics and the House of Technology. Three *statues* also stand on the square: on the southern side, the equestrian statue commemorates *Ferenc Rákóczi II;* this rich aristocrat, Prince of Transylvania, led the 1703–11 war of independence against the Habsburgs and died in 1735 in Rodosto (Tekirdag, Turkey), in exile. To the north, the standing figure is that of *Lajos Kossuth,* the leader of the 1848–49 Hungarian War of Independence and the elected Governor of Hungary. A brilliant speaker and political writer, he died in exile in Turin. The statue is the work of Zsigmond Kisfaludi Strobl (1952). At the northern corner of the Parliament stands the memorial to Mihály Károlyi, the President of the 1918 Hungarian Republic, who was also forced into emigration in 1919.

Southeast of Kossuth Lajos tér, in the direction of the Inner City, *Szabadság tér*—4,300 sq.m. (about one acre)—is only a few steps away. In the centre of the square stands the memorial of the Soviet soldiers who fell during the liberation of the capital. The large eclectic building on the Danube side is the former Stock Exchange, which is now the headquarters of *Hungarian Television.* Opposite to it stands the *National Bank of Hungary,* built in a similar style and also at the beginning of the century (both buildings were designed by Ignác Alpár [1855–1928]). The other building of the National Bank of Hungary, in nearby Rosenberg házaspár utca, a characteristic example of the specifically Hungarian version of Art Nouveau, was built in 1900 by Ödön Lechner.

5

GELLÉRT HILL AND ITS NEIGHBOURHOOD

Rising steeply above the capital, *Gellért Hill* (Gellérthegy) seems from the Danube to be a huge cliff, although it is only 140 metres (430 ft.) above the level of the river. Owing to its exceptional situation, it offers a peerless panorama of the entire city. Up to the end of the nineteenth century this was the limit of the town of Buda, and the hill served as an outpost and fortress of Buda Castle. The plateau is still not fully built over: only on the southern and western slopes can we find villas. The top can be reached on foot in a good quarter of an hour from the Buda end of either Elizabeth or Liberty Bridge. The motor road starts from Elizabeth Bridge, but bus 27 starting at Móricz Zsigmond körtér will also take you to the summit.

The **Citadel,** the fortress on top of the hill, was built between 1850 and 1854 by the despotic Habsburg authorities to control the city after the suppression of the Hungarian War of Independence. The walls in the east-west direction are 200 metres (220 yds.) long, 4 to 6 metres (13–20 ft.) high and at some points 3 metres (10 ft.) thick. In 1897 the Austrian troops left the fortress, and in 1899 the city of Budapest, which bought it, had the walls symbolically demolished—as can still be seen next to the main gate— but then it was again used to house Hungarian soldiers. During the 1944–45 siege it was from the Citadel (and from Castle Hill) that the encircled German troops kept the city under gunfire until their final surrender. Today the Citadel serves as a look-out terrace and has a restaurant. The former barracks have been converted into a tourist hostel.

Looking northward from the hilltop the Buda hills and the Pilis mountains can be seen. On the Buda side, we can almost look into the streets of Castle Hill and recognize the southern fortifications of the Royal Palace. Directly below us we see the slopes of the former Tabán district converted into a park. The Tabán was once a Turkish suburb of small houses. All the Danube bridges are visible; the nearest are Elizabeth Bridge and Liberty Bridge; towards the south we see Petőfi Bridge and the Southern Railway Bridge, towards the north the Chain Bridge, Margaret Bridge, Árpád Bridge and the Northern Railway Bridge. On

The Citadel with the Liberation Monument and the Lágymányos housing estate

the Pest side the dome of the Parliament building dominates the view, with the churches of the Inner City further south; eastwards the mass of houses of Pest extend far over the plain. In the distance we can discern the hills encircling the city, the relics of the former Danube "terraces". Immediately in front of us, a direct continuation of Liberty Bridge, lie the former large residential districts of Ferencváros (Francis Town) and Józsefváros (Joseph Town). To the south, in Buda, the domed building at the foot of the hill is the *Gellért Hotel and Spa;* the blocks further down along the Danube belong to the University of Technology. Still further new housing estates rise from the level districts of Lágymányos and Kelenföld, and on Csepel Island we see the smoking chimneys of the largest Hungarian industrial plant, the Csepel Works.

The **Liberation Monument** (the work of Zsigmond Kisfaludi Strobl) was erected in 1947 to commemorate the liberation of the country and in honour of the soldiers of the liberating Soviet Army. The female figure

View of Buda from the Gellért Hill

The Tabán district with St. Catherine's Church

holding the palm of victory together with the pedestal is 40 metres (132 ft.) high. In front of it is the statue of a Soviet soldier; of the two accessory figures one vanquishes the symbolic figure of destruction and devastation, the other one raises high the torch of progress. The names of fallen Soviet soldiers are carved on the pedestal.

On the southern and western slopes below the Citadel the *Jubilee Park* was completed in 1965–66; from here the view extends to the semicircle of the Buda hills. Of the statues in the park mention must be made of István Kiss's relief "Budapest" and of Ferenc Medgyess's work "St. Gerard's (Gellért's) Fountain" standing in the lower end of the park.

Walking down from Gellért Hill towards Elizabeth Bridge, we come to the statue of *Bishop St. Gerard* (Gellért) standing on the hillside. It was at this spot that the Venetian missionary died a martyr's death early in the eleventh century. In the little district of Tabán, which lies at the northern foot of Gellért Hill and consists of only a few streets, the beautiful eighteenth-century Baroque *St. Catherine Church* and the fifteenth-century *Rác (Imre) Baths* are the most outstanding monuments. At the Buda end of the Elizabeth Bridge the domed building of the *Rudas Baths* dating from Turkish times is worth attention. From the Middle Ages up to the 1930s this was a densely populated district with hundreds of small houses. Here lived the men who built the Danube ferry-boats, the ferrymen and the coachmen; the vineyard-workers came to live here and later it became a Turkish settlement. A large park has taken the place of the houses which were pulled down. Before leaving the Tabán district and going on to the Chain Bridge along the chestnut avenue running northwards on the Danube bank, let us stop for a minute in front of the house at *No. 1–3 Apród utca,* which is now the Museum of Medical History. In this eighteenth-century building was born—and is buried—Ignác Semmelweis (1818–1865), one of the pioneers of the fight against puerperal fever.

6

THE DANUBE BANK OF BUDA; ÓBUDA, AQUINCUM

In olden times an important Roman road ran from today's Chain Bridge towards Aquincum. In the Middle Ages this road became the main street of the Buda suburb of Water Town and from there it led to the queens' town, Óbuda. It is still called *Fő utca* (meaning Main Street), and it starts from *Clark Ádám tér* at the Buda end of the Chain Bridge. From the symbolic "0" kilometre stone (by Miklós Borsos) in this square the distances of Hungarian main roads are measured.

The Batthyány tér and its neighbourhood. A few years ago, with a station of the east-west Metro line and the terminal of the northern suburban railway, *Batthyány tér* became an important traffic junction.

St. Anne's Church (built by Máté Nepauer, Kristóf and Mihály Hamon, 1740–62), which faces the square, is a beautiful example of Italian Baroque ecclesiastical architecture introduced into Hungary by Austrian artists. The two towers, topped by ornate spires, and the portal with its allegoric statues dominate the exterior. The interior is covered by an oval-shaped dome. The pillared high altar with its group of statues also dates from the eighteenth century.

The houses at *Nos. 3* and *4* are also ancient monuments. The latter was an inn around 1770, and was the starting-point of the Vienna stage-coaches. The theatrical performances and balls of Buda were also held here. On the northern side there formerly stood a monastery and hospital, its church built by Franciscan friars between 1731 and 1756; later on it became a convent of Elizabethan nuns. The carved benches and the groups of statues on the altars are particularly beautiful. In front of the building stands the statue of Ferenc Kölcsey, author of the Hungarian National Anthem.

A house in Corvin tér

Batthyány tér: St. Anne's Church

A few minutes' walk northwards in *Fő utca* takes us to the building at *No. 82–86*. In a little park stands the Turkish dome of the *Király Baths*, built between 1566 and 1570 on the orders of Pashas Arslan and Sokoli Mustapha. To the original Turkish building neo-Classical wings have been added; inside, the reconstruction after the Second World War revealed some Baroque arcaded corridors built when the building was renovated in the eighteenth century, as well as a neo-Classical pillared courtyard. The baths got their name from their owners in the early nineteenth century, the König family (König meaning "king", in Hungarian *király*). Only a few steps away, at *No. 20* Bem utca is the *Foundry Museum* (see p. 127), and a little further on, at *No. 14* Mecset utca, there is a Turkish monument, the *tomb of Gül Baba*.

The tomb of Gül Baba

The Lukács and Császár Baths. Continuing our walk and crossing Mártírok útja, the main boulevard of Buda, through an underground passage, we are in Frankel Leó utca, where, at *No. 25–29*, we find the Lukács spa and swimming pool, and, at *No. 31–33*, the Császár baths. These small bathing establishments grew at the beginning of the nineteenth century on the level land between the hills and the river Danube. As early as the Middle Ages, charitable knights had a hospital here, and later the Turks added baths. However, in Turkish times the abundant hot springs were mainly used to work the gunpowder-mills. At present the baths, fed by 17 springs and with a temperature of 17–50°C (60–122°F), provide relief and cure for patients suffering from rheumatism, arthritis, inflammations and muscular diseases. On the left side of Frankel Leó utca, the Mill Pond (Malom-tó) collects the water of some of the hot-water springs.

The *Lukács Baths* were built by József Hild in 1842 in neo-Classical style. The tablets on the walls of the inner court have been placed there by grateful patients who were cured here. The original Turkish bath adjoins the main building. The Turkish bath hall of the *Császár Baths* is surrounded by neo-Classical and Romantic buildings. The curative effect of the water was already known to the Romans. The bath hall was built in 1571–72 by Pasha Sokollu Mustapha. The other parts of the building were constructed in 1829 to the designs of József Hild. Next to the old bath rises the *Komjádi sports swimming pool*, completed in 1976. Along the opposite side of the narrowing street is the long building of a former hospital for rheumatics. The new trade union sanatorium built in 1968–70 rises above it on Rose Hill (Rózsadomb).

Óbuda. Budapest's largest housing estate is being built on the site of the single-storey houses of this formerly rural district. Only a few remainders of the one-time Roman legionaries' town, of the medieval Chapter seat and of the queens' palace could be excavated; all of these were destroyed during the Turkish occupation and, after 1686, settlers founded a new town on the site.

In 1872 Óbuda was united with Buda and Pest. The *Árpád Bridge,* completed in 1950, is the longest bridge in Budapest—it stretches for almost two kilometres (1¼ m.), together with its approaches, and it directly links Óbuda and Pest. At the Buda end of the bridge large-scale reconstruction has been finished, but a group of historical monuments is being left intact as a relic of the past: the eighteenth-century *Baroque palace* at No. 1 Fő tér and its immediate surroundings preserve the atmosphere of the one-time town district. Collections of the town's history can be seen in the palace, while a nearby single-storey building (No. 7 Laktanya utca) houses a permanent *exhibition* by the sculptor *Imre Varga*. In *Flórián tér,* under the approach road to Árpád Bridge, a museum of Roman stonework finds offers a special sight. Also located here are the remains of a former military baths.

Aquincum. 3 kilometres (1.8 m.) to the north of Flórián tér, in the centre of Óbuda, can be seen the excavated ruins of this former Roman town. The excavations are along Szentendrei út, near the station of the suburban express railway which starts at Batthyány tér.

The town was founded in the first century A.D. by the Roman legions which had occupied the region they called Pannonia, and which is today's Transdanubia. The military settlement was situated on the site of today's Óbuda, to the south of Árpád Bridge. Aquincum was a civilian town surrounded by walls, with aqueducts, sewers and paved streets. Artisans, tradesmen and vine-growers lived here, but in the fourth century the repeated attacks of the Barbarians forced the population to leave the city. Gradually even the walls disappeared; the foundations came to light only during excavations which, though started at the end of the eighteenth century, have only recently become regular and continuous.

The entrance to the *field of ruins* is near the railway line. The first important monument there is the remains of the basilica of the Forum. Beyond the east-west main road vast public baths have been unearthed. We can recognize the cashier's booth, the dressing-rooms and further on the cold, lukewarm and hot-water pools. The heating system was installed under the floor, which was supported by columns, and in the passages of the hollow walls. The baths were fed by a medicinal spring. Nearby stood the great markethall, and to the east the main part of another bath, a swimming pool 6 by 4.5 metres (21 by 15 ft.) in area, and next to it a large Roman-style dwelling-house, with rooms opening out from a colonnaded courtyard. The owner must have been a rich man, because the house had a separate main building, the mosaic floor of which, depicting wrestlers,

Old houses in Óbuda

can be seen today under a protective covering. Behind the mosaic-decorated baths the cave-like Mithras temple is worth seeing. The cult of Mithras, the light-god of the people of the Near East, was widespread in Pannonia.

In the halls of the *museum* the most precious finds unearthed during the excavations are displayed. In Hall 1 a map shows the location of Pannonia within the Roman Empire and that of Aquincum in the province of Pannonia. The carved stones exhibited are remains of altars and statues of gods. In Hall 2 to the right, inter-

Aquincum—the amphitheatre

esting items are the *terra sigillata* vessels and bronze statuettes that found their way to Pannonia from different parts of the Empire. These items include a lovely bronze figure representing a black slave-boy. The instruments put on display were used by Roman land surveyors and builders of roads. Hall 3 is reserved for the relics of handicrafts and trade. Notable among these are a wooden casket that have come down to us intact and a potter's kiln. Hall 4 (to the left) contains the mementoes of art and cultural life. Unique among the objects to be seen here is a water organ. Religious life in the Roman period is presented in Hall 5. Here mention should be made of an altar dedicated to Mithras, which has survived intact, and of the cultic objects of the early Christians.

The *civilian amphitheatre* stood on the other side of today's railway line; the 53-metre (58 yds.) long elliptical arena could hold 5,000 to 6,000 spectators. On the way back from Aquincum you will find it worthwhile to stop and have a look at the ruins of the *amphitheatre of the military town,* in Nagyszombat utca, a side-turning off the main road. Built in the second century, this is one of the largest amphitheatres built by the Romans outside Italy; the length of the arena is 89 metres (98 yds.); it could hold an audience of 13,000. On the side facing the hills, the original height and the shape of the cages where the wild beasts were held are perceptible, thanks to recent reconstruction. Another significant monument of this period in Óbuda is the *Roman military baths* under the house at *No. 3* Flórián tér, with their heating area still intact and their cold and hot-water pools. Not far from here, on the corner of Meggyfa utca and Vihar utca, can be found in the courtyard of a school building the most beautiful intact *mosaic floor* in Pannonia: made by an Italian master from extremely fine marble grains, it depicts a scene of the Hercules myth.

Though not containing any Roman finds, the Department of Modern History of the *Budapest History Museum* (108 Kiscelli utca) should be mentioned here as it is also in Óbuda. It presents the history of the capital, and its Baroque building, a former monastery, is in itself worth seeing.

MARGARET ISLAND

Árpád Bridge to the north, and Margaret Bridge to the south connect Margaret Island with the city. The island is 2.5 km (1.4 m.) long, 500 m (550 yds.) wide, and it covers 225 acres. In contrast to similar islands in other great cities, this one has not been built over, but has remained a huge park in the heart of the city. In the Middle Ages cloisters were built on the "Rabbits' Island", as it was then called; at the beginning of the nineteenth century members of the royal family living in Buda transformed it into a landscape garden. By the turn of the century it had become a health resort owing to its therapeutic springs.

There is only one motor road which runs the length of the island (but open only for buses); otherwise there are only footpaths. Century-old trees, quiet walks, a flower-garden, romantic ruins and a little game-reserve offer relaxation to people tired of the noise of the city, old and young alike. At the Margaret Bridge entrance to the island the visitor sees a *fountain* and the *Centenary Monument* (by István Kiss, 1972) erected on the hundredth anniversary of the union of Pest and Buda. The *Pioneers' Stadium* is a children's sports establishment. On the Buda side of the island is the *Alfréd Hajós Sports Swimming Pool,* with an indoor pool 33.3 m (37 yds.) long and two open-air ones of 33.3 and 50 m (55 yds.); further on, in the centre of the island, are the *Palatinus Outdoor Baths.* The latter occupy an area of 17.5 acres and the three pools are filled with therapeutic water. In front of it we find the city's most beautiful rosegarden. Not far away, on the *open-air stage* next to the water tower, opera, operetta and ballet performances are held. There is an *open-air cinema* which functions in summer and nearby we find the *Tennis Stadium.*

The most significant ancient monument on the island is the ruin of a thirteenth-century *convent of Dominican nuns* near the open-air theatre. The convent was founded by King Béla IV, who built up the country again after the Mongol invasion (1241–42) and is therefore sometimes called the second founder of the State. His daughter Margaret came to live in the convent in 1251 at the age of eleven. She was later canonized and the island now bears her name. A marble plaque in the

The Danube with Margaret Island as seen from Margaret Bridge

nave of the church ruins indicates the spot where she was buried. A few steps to the north of the convent ruins we see the *chapel of the medieval Premonstratensian monastery*. In its tower hangs the oldest bell in Hungary. It was made in the fifteenth century and discovered intact not many years ago among the roots of a tree torn out by a storm. Around the chapel, along the promenade, we find statues of the most eminent representatives of Hungarian literature and arts. Walking to the north we reach the *Grand Hotel, Ramada* and the *Thermal* spa hotel. At the northern end of the island the

Romantic Margaret Island

exotic plants and the artificial waterfall and a charming *rock garden* delight the tired sightseer. (To be approached by car only from Árpád Bridge through the car park around the hotels.)

HŐSÖK TERE (HEROES' SQUARE), THE MUSEUM OF FINE ARTS

Approach: from Buda and the Inner City, buses 1 and 4; also by the old Underground line.

Hősök tere lies at the end of the 2.5 km (1.4 m.) long Népköztársaság útja, the avenue which starts at Bajcsy-Zsilinszky út. In the centre of the square stands the Millenary Monument, to the left is the Museum of Fine Arts and to the right the imposing building of the Art Gallery (Műcsarnok). In the centre we see the Memorial of Hungarian Heroes, a 47-ton monolith.

The construction of the **Millenary Monument** was begun in 1896, the thousandth anniversary of the Conquest of the country by the Hungarians. It was designed by the architect Albert Schickedanz and the sculptor György Zala. The centre of the monument is a 36-metre (160 ft.) high column with a winged genius on top and the statues of the conquering Magyar chief Árpád and of the chiefs of the other six tribes on the pedestal. Behind these there is a semicircular colonnade with the statues of the most outstanding Hungarian kings, princes and commanders between the columns. From left to right: St. Stephen, the founder of the State, Ladislas I, Coloman, Andrew II and Béla IV, kings of the House of Árpád; Charles Robert and Louis I known as the Great of the Angevin dynasty; János Hunyadi, the hero of the wars against the Turks, and King Matthias; then Gábor Bethlen, István Bocskai, Imre Thököly and Ferenc Rákóczi II, princes of Transylvania, and finally Lajos Kossuth, the leader of the 1848–49 War of Independence. Below the bronze statues reliefs commemorate historic events. On top of the semicircle there are four symbolic statues: Work and Wealth on the left, two chariots depicting War and Peace in the centre, and Honour and Glory on the right.

The eclectic building of the **Museum of Fine Arts,** completed in 1906, was designed by Albert Schickedanz and Fülöp Herzog. Above the wide flight of stairs, eight plus four Corinthian columns support the tympanum, the relief of which is a copy of the group on the western pediment of the Temple of Zeus at Olympia and depicts the fight of Centaurs and Lapiths. Various historical styles characterize the interior halls.

The eclectic building of the **Art Gallery,** reminiscent of a Greek temple, stands opposite the Museum of Fine Arts and was designed by the same artists. Built in 1895, its most characteristic feature is the coloured ceramic ornamentation. The National Fine Arts Exhibition is held here every other year, as are other temporary exhibitions, large and small. Near Hősök tere Dózsa György út widens out; parades and popular meetings are held here. In the section behind the Art Gallery rises the grandstand; its reliefs by the sculptor Sándor Mikus depict work. Not far from it we find the *memorial of the 1919 Hungarian Soviet Republic* (by István Kiss, 1969), and immediately behind the Art Gallery, a *statue of Lenin* (by Pál Pátzay, 1965).

When the **Museum of Fine Arts** was established, the Hungarian government bought collections from rich aristocratic families and prelates. The collection has since been enriched by further purchases and donations.

The collections in the Museum comprise an Egyptian department, a Greek and Roman collection, a Gallery of Old Masters, an exhibition of Old Statues, a Modern Foreign Gallery, a collection of Modern Sculptures, a collection of Twentieth Century Art, and a collection of Drawings. Hungarian works of art are exhibited in the *Hungarian National Gallery* (see p. 110).

The *Egyptian Exhibition* displays relics of the Egyptian cult of the dead—mummies, painted coffins, cult objects and vessels—and illustrates the development of Egyptian culture grouped into seven great historic periods. Working tools, vessels, fragments of painted reliefs, gravestones, statues and papyrus fragments are exhibited. The most precious pieces are the limestone statue of the Pharaoh Sheshonk, some beautiful Apis bulls and relics of the later, Ptolemaean and Roman periods.

The oldest pieces of the *Greek and Roman collection* date from the Late Stone Age and the Early Bronze Age; note, for instance, two marble statues of women from the third millennium B.C. You will also find several characteristic pieces from the Cretan and Mycenaean periods, relics of seventh and sixth-century vase painting, among them a few extremely rare Cyprus vases, Greek terracotta statues from the Classical period of the sixth and fifth centuries; and marble statues from the fourth century. From the Hellenistic period the most important piece is the marble statuette of the

City Park with the Millenary Monument and a carriage of the "Little Underground" from the end of the last century, in use in this form until 1973

"Budapest Dancer" and, from the third century, the "Tyche", the protecting divinity of the town of Antioch; but you can also see relics of the late Etruscan and Italian periods, as well as terracotta reliefs from Roman villas of the first century, and finally, from the end of the Republican period and from the Imperial period, marble statues of mythological figures, relics of small Roman sculptures and goldsmiths' works.

The Gallery of Old Masters is the largest and most valuable collection in the museum. Outside Spain, the Hermitage collection is the only one in Europe richer in

Spanish paintings than that in Budapest. The outstanding pieces are El Greco's "Mary Magdalene", "Disrobing of Christ", "Study of a Man" and "The Agony in the Garden"; from the seventeenth century there are works by Bartolomé Esteban Murillo, Francisco de Zurbarán, Jusepe de Ribera, and Diego Velázquez. A few world-famous paintings by Goya are also exhibited here: "The Water Seller", "The Knife-Grinder" and the portraits of the wife of Céan Bermúdez and of the Minister of Justice Caballero.

The *Italian* collection contains a comparatively large number of fourteenth-century works; few museums outside Italy possess so many of these. Noteworthy are Ghirlandaio's figure of "St. Stephen", Bellini's portrait of Caterina Cornaro, Crivelli's Madonna, Giorgione's and Sebastiano del Piombo's male portraits, works by Titian, Tintoretto and Veronese, Raphael's "Pietro Bembo" and "The Esterházy Madonna", a Madonna by Correggio, paintings by Magnasco, Canaletto, and Tiepolo's large "St. James the Great".

Of the valuable *Dutch and Flemish* collection we should mention Pieter Bruegel the Elder's "St John the Baptist Preaching", a "Crucifixion" by Memling, Gerard David's "Nativity", some later works by Rembrandt, among them "The Old Rabbi", as well as paintings by Vermeer van Delft, Frans Hals, Ostade, Van Goyen, Jan Steen, Rubens and Van Dyck.

When visiting the early *German* collection we must look at the "Three Magi" by the Master of the Viennese Adoration, the "Cloaked Virgin" by the Cologne Master of the Life of the Virgin, Holbein's "Death of the Virgin", Albrecht Dürer's male portrait, the works of Hans Baldung Grien and Albrecht Altdorfer and numerous paintings by Lucas Cranach. As to Baroque paintings, mention must be made of the works of *Austrian* artists, mainly of Maulbertsch and Kremser-Schmidt. Viennese Biedermeier painting is represented by the works of some well-known masters (Eybl, Waldmüller).

The collection of *British* paintings contains works by William Hogarth, Joshua Reynolds, Thomas Gainsborough, John Opie, Henry Raeburn and John Constable; the *French* school is represented by Nicolas Poussin, Simon Vouet, Philippe de Champaigne, Claude Lorraine, Jean-Baptiste-Siméon Chardin and Jean-Baptiste Greuze.

In the *Modern Foreign Gallery* the most significant

pieces are nineteenth-century French paintings by Eugène Delacroix, Charles Daubigny, Constant Troyon, Camille Corot, Gustave Courbet and Camille Pissarro. You can see here Manet's world-famous "Lady with Fan" (Jeanne Duval), Claude Monet's "The Harbour at Trouville"; "Blossoming Appletrees" and "Fishing Boats", an early snowscape by Paul Gauguin, a portrait of a girl by Auguste Renoir, works by Paul Cézanne, Henri de Toulouse-Lautrec, Paul Gauguin, Pierre Bonnard, Pierre Puvis de Chavanne, and Maurice Denis, as well as Kokoschka's early masterpiece "Veronica".

The latest exhibition put on show in the Museum is the one entitled *Twentieth Century Art*. In the constantly increasing collection are works of Marc Chagall, Pablo Picasso, Oskar Kokoschka, Jean Arp, Theo van Doesburg, Fred Forbat, Renato Guttuso, Le Corbusier, S. Kolos-Vary, Amerigo Tot, Victor Vasarely, Fritz Wotruba and others.

The *Exhibition of Old Statues* displays works from the fourth to the eighteenth century; its most outstanding section contains the Italian acquisitions, statues and decorative stone carvings from the twelfth to the sixteenth century. Verrocchio's "Christ" and Leonardo da Vinci's "Warrior on Rearing Horse" are world famous.

From the fourteenth to sixteenth-century *German* school we must mention a wooden statue of "The Virgin and Child" by a Swabian master, wooden statues from the workshop of Tilmann Riemenschneider, a "Calvary Group" and a "Crucifix" by southern Tyrolean masters, and a "Mary with the Infant Jesus" on a Gothic pedestal from the workshop of Veit Stoss.

The French, Spanish, Dutch and English material is very rich, too, and some important works of the seventeenth and eighteenth-century Italian, German and Austrian schools can also be seen.

The *Collection of Modern Sculpture* contains works by nineteenth-century European sculptors. The most interesting pieces are Auguste Rodin's "Eternal Spring", "Bronze Age" and "Nereids", as well as important works by Meunier, Maillol and Meštrović.

The *Collection of Drawings* amounts to almost 100,000 and its most valuable possessions are shown in temporary exhibitions, such as original works by Italian, German and Dutch masters. The most outstanding masterpieces are three Leonardo studies and fifteen works by Rembrandt; the Italian masters are also represented by the works of Raphael, Correggio, Veronese, Tintoretto and many others. (Please note that the various collections can be seen at different times, which means that several visits are required to see the whole museum.)

9

THE CITY PARK (VÁROSLIGET)

Behind Hősök tere lies the City Park, the largest park on the Pest side, covering exactly one square kilometre (0.4 sq.m.). The area was once part of the sand and grass-covered Field of Rákos, where in former days the Diets and the national markets were held; at the beginning of the last century it was converted into a park. By the turn of the century it had already become a place of entertainment popular with all layers of society: members of the aristocracy drove out here in their carriages and exercised their horses; the middle classes came here for a day out; and here the workers organized their meetings and their May Day demonstrations.

Behind Hősök tere and the Museum of Fine Arts, on Állatkerti körút (Zoo Boulevard) is the *Zoo* with the *Municipal Circus* next to it; further down is the *Amusement Park* and on the opposite side are the *Széchenyi Baths*. Immediately behind Hősök tere is an artificial lake: used for rowing in summer, it becomes an artificial skating rink in winter. Around the lake there are a wooded park and a children's playground; on a small island in the lake we find an interesting group of buildings, Vajdahunyad Castle.

Vajdahunyad Castle was built between 1896 and 1908; its various parts illustrate the different styles of Hungarian architecture. It was designed by Ignác Alpár, and derived its name from the wing facing the lake, which is an imitation of the Castle of Vajdahunyad in Transylvania, the family castle of János Hunyadi, the hero of the Turkish wars, which was built in its present form in the fifteenth century (today Hunedoara, Rumania). A Gothic gate leads to the courtyard. To the left are Romanesque buildings; the chapel uses motifs of the famous thirteenth-century Benedictine abbey at Ják in Western Hungary, the most beautiful surviving relic of Romanesque architecture in the country. The chapel is flanked by a pseudo-

The City Park Lake and Vajdahunyad Castle

medieval ambulatory with a corner turret. The buildings facing the lake are imitations of a castle-wall and a feudal castle.

On the opposite side, the outstanding structure among the Gothic group of buildings is the copy of the castle-tower of Segesvár in Transylvania (now Sighişoară, Rumania). Inside there is a Gothic courtyard with some early Renaissance elements.

The largest façade facing the courtyard was built in Baroque style. Opposite is the *statue of Anonymus,* his face hidden in his monk's hood symbolizing the fact that the identity of the thirteenth-century chronicler is unknown—even today we do not know much more about him than that he worked at the royal court. His work "Gesta Hungarorum", written in Latin and based on earlier chronicles now lost, contains the Hunnish-Hungarian cycle of legends as well as the history of the Magyar Conquest and of the first kings of the House of Árpád. (The statue is the work of Miklós Ligeti, 1903.)

The **Agricultural Museum** is housed in Vajdahunyad Castle. It presents the various branches of Hungarian agriculture: the breeding of domestic animals, the life of the shepherds in the Hungarian Puszta and their handicraft, horse-breeding, the skeleton of the world-famous race-horse Kincsem, the fauna of the forests, the history of forestry and sylviculture. The hunting exhibition presents the wildlife of Hungarian forests and waters, and a rich collection of antlers. At the fishing exhibition you can learn about old fishing implements, the fishes that live in Hungarian waters, and modern fishing methods. There are also interesting exhibitions on viticulture with a collection of wine-presses and an exhibition on the mechanization of agriculture.

Further walks in the City Park

At the beginning of Állatkerti körút *(No. 2)* is the *Gundel Restaurant,* famous for its cuisine where, in the summer, one can eat out of doors in the pleasant garden.

Next to it are the *Municipal Zoological and Botanical Gardens.* The rich collection of animals are kept, as far as possible, in their natural environment and reared according to the most modern scientific principles. (See p. 96)

Beside the Zoo we find the large modern building of the *Municipal Circus,* completed in 1970. Next to it is the *Amusement Park* (Vidám Park), popular with the young people of Budapest and foreign visitors alike for its varied entertainments, which include a scenic railway, a game-room, etc. There is also a small *Amusement Park* for children.

Opposite the Zoo stand the *Széchenyi Medicinal Baths and Swimming Pool,* erected between 1909 and 1913 and enlarged in 1926. The thermal water of 70°C (158°F) gushes from a 1,250 metre (4,100 ft.) deep artesian well. Opposite the main entrance stands a statue of the noted geologist Vilmos Zsigmondy, who discovered the first thermal spring in the City Park in 1877.

Passing the Art Gallery on Hősök tere we reach the southern parts of the City Park. At the intersection of the lakeside promenade and the little bridge leading to the island the *statue of George Washington* catches the eye. It was erected in 1906 by Hungarians living in the United States at the same time as a statue of the great nineteenth-century Hungarian patriot Lajos Kossuth was raised in Cleveland, Ohio.

Heading east through the park, we reach *Petőfi Hall,* which was converted from a former pavilion in the Budapest International Fair into a youth cultural and recreational centre.

The *Transport Museum* stands on the corner of Állatkerti körút and Május 1. út (First of May Road), bordering the Park on the east. It was built in 1896 to the plans of Krisztián Ulrich on the occasion of the Millenary celebrations. Its domed building and the greater part of its collection were destroyed during the Second World War. Since it was rebuilt new exhibits are on display, showing the history of bridges and of rail, road, water and air transport. A new wing was added to it in 1987.

In the southern half of City Park we find children's playgrounds, a small garden of statues and a botanical garden.

SZENT ISTVÁN KÖRÚT, THE BASILICA, NÉPKÖZTÁRSASÁG ÚTJA

By walking along the Great Boulevard we shall get acquainted with the busiest and most densely populated districts of the city. Let us start from the *Pest end of Margaret Bridge*. Built from 1872 to 1876 to the design of the French firm of Gouin, Margaret Bridge was the second permanent bridge in Budapest, after the Chain Bridge. The most tragic event of its history occurred in October 1944, when German mines blew it up while it was full of vehicles and pedestrians. The bridge was rebuilt in 1948–49.

The Pest bridgehead is the starting point of the Great Boulevard, the first part of which is called Szent István körút. To the north of the bridgehead there is a children's playground; to the south we find an impressive modern building, the *headquarters of the Hungarian Socialist Workers' Party* with the *statue of Marx and Engels* in front of it (by György Segesdy, 1971).

The huge eclectic buildings along Szent István körút—today a busy thoroughfare and an important shopping district with many restaurants, pastry-shops and espressos—were built about the turn of the century. Conspicuous is the domed *Comedy Theatre* (Vígszínház). In front of it two busts represent Sándor Petőfi, the great poet of the 1848–49 War of Independence, and Miklós Zrínyi, the seventeenth-century Hungarian general and epic poet. The theatre was opened in 1896 to give a home to modern drama.

To the south of Szent István körút side streets lead to the administrative and government district, and to the north to new residential quarters. This section of the Great Boulevard ends in the busy traffic junction of Marx tér. On this square is the main entrance of the *Western Railway Station*. The building of the present station was erected in 1874–77 in the place of the first Hungarian railway station, built in 1846. Designed by the Gustave Eiffel firm of Paris, the iron roofing is typical of the architectural design of the building. In 1978–80, the whole railway station was modernized. A subway in the square leads to the Metro stop (the north-south or No. 3 line). From Marx tér, Váci út, lined with the factories and leading from the capital to the Czechoslovak border, branches out towards the

The Great Boulevard: the "Hungária" palace

north, whilst Bajcsy-Zsilinszky út, which leads to the Little Boulevard, branches out to the south.

From Marx tér, the Great Boulevard continues as *Lenin körút,* intersects *Népköztársaság útja,* then later on the busiest shopping street, *Rákóczi út,* which is full of department stores, and continues as *József körút,* and, later, as *Ferenc körút,* before reaching Petőfi Bridge.

The Basilica (St Stephen's Church), the most impressive building of Bajcsy-Zsilinszky út, has its main façade towards the Danube; from Bajcsy-Zsilinszky út all we see are its semicircular chancel walls. The monumental neo-Renaissance church was designed by two well-known masters of the Hungarian architecture of the turn of the century, József Hild and Miklós Ybl, and was built between 1851 and 1905. The area of the church, a Greek cross with a dome and two steeples, is 86 by 55 m (285 by 183 ft.). The dome, burned down during the war and rebuilt in 1948–49, is the highest among the churches of Budapest—96 m. (314 ft.)—, the same height as the dome of the Parliament building. Statues of Latin Fathers of the Church stand in the ground-floor niches, the four Evangelists are in the protruding niches of the pillars, and the statues of the twelve Apostles stand above the semicircular colonnade of the chancel.

The vestibule of the main entrance is shaped like a triumphal arch. The relief of the tympanum above the two Corinthian half-columns depicts Our Lady, the Patroness of Hungary, with Hungarian saints; the wall above the main entrance is decorated with a relief of the Hungarian king St. Stephen, and a mosaic depicting the resurrection of Christ. The works of significant Hungarian artists of the period, among them Mór Than, Bertalan Székely, and Gyula Benczúr, ornament the inside of the church and the chancel; the statues of Hungarian saints—St. Elizabeth, St. Gerard, St. Emeric, and St. Ladislas holding his sword high—stand near the inside main pillar of the dome. The mosaics of the dome were designed by Károly Lotz, a famous Hungarian fresco-painter of the turn of the century. St. Stephen's statue on the main altar is the work of Alajos Stróbl; the five bronze reliefs of the chancel illustrate scenes from the life of the first Hungarian king.

Népköztársaság útja (the Avenue of the People's Republic) starts out at Bajcsy-Zsilinszky út, opposite the Basilica. This beautiful, two-and-a-half kilometre

The Opera House, inner staircase

(1.5 m.) long avenue was constructed at the end of the last century almost simultaneously from both ends; the resulting row of buildings, mainly neo-Renaissance and neo-Baroque, thus gives an impression of unity. Miklós Ybl, the most eminent Hungarian architect of the period, supervised the planning of the avenue, which is at once the most dignified and the most harmonious eclectic architectural *ensemble* of the country. At the intersection of the avenue—originally called Sugárút (Radial Avenue)—and the Great Boulevard, an octagonal square was created; this is today's *November 7. tér* (its old name was the Octagon); from here onwards tree-lined pedestrian walks break the avenue into three lanes. Further on, after we pass the *Kodály körönd,* we come to a part of the avenue lined with villas and gardens; the avenue ends at *Hősök tere* (Heroes' Square) with the *Millenary Monument.*

The continent's first *Underground Railway* was built between 1894 and 1896 under today's Népköztársaság útja to honour the millennium of the conquest of the country by the Hungarians. The 4.5 km (2.6 m.) long so-called "cut-and-cover" railway underwent reconstruction in 1973. Its original route was lengthened and today it connects the Inner City with the new housing estate at Mexikói út.

Of the many noteworthy buildings of *Népköztársaság útja,* we call attention to some in particular. The interesting features of the richly decorated eclectic house at *No. 2* are staged balconies looking onto József Attila utca. A plaque was placed on this building to commemorate the politician Endre Bajcsy-Zsilinszky (1886–1944), the leader of the bourgeois wing of the Hungarian anti-Fascist movement, who died a martyr's death. It is also worthwhile to cast a glance at the house *No. 3,* built between 1884 and 1886; its three-storey façade is ornamented by balustrated balconies, its first floor, above the two sidewindows and the central window, by statues; the staircase fresco illustrating Roman bacchanalia is the work of Károly Lotz. The gate of the house at *No. 5* is decorated with statues and marble columns; on the building at *No. 7* you will see frieze reliefs and medallions; two caryatids adorn the gate of *No. 9;* the sgraffito-covered courtyard of *No. 12* is an enchanting sight with its lovely ornamental fountain. The building at *No. 22* is the **Hungarian State Opera.** It was built between 1875 and 1884 to the designs of Miklós Ybl in Italian neo-Renaissance style. The balcony on the

Népköztársaság útja at Kodály körönd

façade has baluster railings, with an arcaded driveway underneath. In the niches on both sides of the driveway stand the statues (by Alajos Stróbl) of *Ferenc Liszt,* the most famous Hungarian composer of the nineteenth century, and *Ferenc Erkel,* creator of Hungarian national opera and the first director of the Opera House. The statues on the corner projections, between the Corinthian half-columns, represent Terpsichore, Erato, Thalia and Melpomene, the Muses of dance, love-poetry, comedy and tragedy. The vaults of the driveway are ornamented with sgraffiti. *The statues of great composers on the façade* were renovated in 1966; these represent from left to right: Monteverdi, Scarlatti, Gluck, Mozart, Beethoven, Rossini, Donizetti, Glinka, Wagner, Verdi, Gounod, Bizet, Moussorgsky, Tchaikovsky, Moniuszko and Smetana. The allegorical frescoes in the vestibule were painted by Bertalan Székely, the ones on the ceiling of the main staircase by Mór Than, the stone carvings were made by Alajos Stróbl, Gyula Donáth and György Kiss. On the landing of the staircase stands the statue of Miklós Ybl. The fresco in the centre of the ceiling of the three-storey high, horseshoe-shaped auditorium was painted by Károly Lotz: it represents a serene Olympus with Apollo in the centre. The ceremonial box is decorated with Gyula Donáth's dancing figures, and the ceiling of the salon behind it with Mór Than's paintings. The full reconstruction of the building was completed in 1984, to coincide with the centenary of its opening.

In addition to the Opera House, the capital has a second opera house, the *Erkel Theatre* (in Köztársaság tér, off Rákóczi út). This theatre, originally completed in 1911, and now seating 2,500 spectators, was rebuilt as a modern opera house and concert hall in the course of reconstruction work after the war. An ensemble, well-known all over Europe, performs in both opera houses.

The building at *No. 25,* opposite the Opera House, the work of the well-known Hungarian architect Ödön Lechner, was built in 1883 in French Renaissance style; it houses the *State Ballet Institute,* in which Hungarian dancers are taught their first steps, and are trained right up to their final graduation, with an artist's diploma.

The next broad cross street, Nagymező utca, and its surrounding area form the capital's theatre district. The *Operetta Theatre* maintains the traditions of the great operettas of Vienna and Budapest. Its neighbour is the *Moulin Rouge,* a night club with floor show and dancing. Nearby we find several other theatres.

Proceeding further on Népköztársaság útja, we note an *Art Nouveau building at No. 39;* it is a department store called Divatcsarnok, its main exhibition hall is decorated with *frescoes by Károly Lotz*. Soon we come to two squares opening off the avenue. To the left, in Jókai tér, we see the statue of *Mór Jókai,* the great Romantic novelist of the nineteenth century (by Alajos Stróbl, 1921), to the right in Liszt Ferenc tér, that of *Endre Ady* (by Géza Csorba, 1960), who in the first two decades of this century brought new life into Hungarian lyric poetry. A few steps from here we find the *Liszt Ferenc Academy of Music.* Before World War II Béla Bartók, Zoltán Kodály, Ernő Dohnányi, and Jenő Hubay were members of its teaching staff, and here first-rate music pedagogues still instruct the composers, performers and music teachers of tomorrow.

From November 7. tér on, Népköztársaság útja becomes wider. In the section after the Great Boulevard, the houses at *Nos. 52, 62* and *67* are characteristic and noteworthy eclectic buildings. In the latter, which is the former Academy of Music, Ferenc Liszt, one of the founders of the Academy and its first director, lived when he stayed in Budapest. His former flat houses the *Ferenc Liszt Memorial Museum. Nos. 69*

Gate on the Kodály körönd

and *71* house the *Academy of Fine Arts*. *No. 69*, built between 1875 and 1877 in Italian Renaissance style, has an ashlar façade with a full-length balcony with Corinthian half-columns and a baluster railing on the first floor. Frescoes by Károly Lotz decorate its vestibule and first-floor corridors. This building houses the State Puppet Theatre as well. *No. 71*, an eclectic building with lovely sgraffiti on its façade, was built in 1875. The predecessor of the Academy of Fine Arts, the first Hungarian school of drawing was founded in 1777, during the reign of Maria Theresa, in the Fortuna Hotel on Castle Hill. In the middle of the nineteenth century the Italian Jacopo Marastoni opened an artists' academy in Pest; among his disciples were the renowned artists Károly Lotz and Bertalan Székely. The present Academy was inaugurated in 1871.

No. 73–75 is the headquarters of the Hungarian State Railway's administration. One of the two copper reliefs commemorates the railwaymen who died in the world wars, the other was erected in 1946, the centenary of the Hungarian railways. The avenue then again widens into a circular open place, the *Kodály körönd* (Circus), bordered by four mansions with arched façades. Under the old plane trees stand four statues: Vak (Blind) Bottyán, an eighteenth-century "kuruc" general of the independence fights of Rákóczi; Miklós Zrínyi, the defender of Szigetvár in 1655; György Szondi, the other legendary hero of the wars against the Turks, and Bálint Balassi, an outstanding lyric poet of the sixteenth century. Of the surrounding buildings, the handsome row of loggias over the double courtyard of *Nos. 83–85* and the wrought-iron gate of the building at *No. 88* are worth a look.

After the Körönd, Népköztársaság útja becomes less closely built up and from Bajza utca onwards the houses are surrounded by gardens: many foreign missions are situated here and it has become the diplomatic district of the capital. At *No. 101* are the premises of the Association of Hungarian Journalists and *No. 103* houses the *Ferenc Hopp Museum of Eastern Asiatic Art*. The capital's most beautiful avenue ends in the artistically composed Hősök tere.

11

THE NATIONAL MUSEUM, THE MUSEUM OF APPLIED ARTS

The **Hungarian National Museum** was founded in 1802 by Count Ferenc Széchényi; its neo-Classical building was erected between 1837 and 1847 to the design of Mihály Pollack on the present Múzeum körút, which at that time was the city border. The group of zinc statues on the tympanum of the façade is the work of the Milanese sculptor Raffaello Monti and the Munich artist Schaller. A wide flight of stairs takes the visitor to the colonnaded vestibule, where a memorial plaque recalls that the mass meeting of March 15, 1848—the prelude to the revolution—was held here. The Museum is surrounded by a picturesque garden with statues commemorating Hungarian scientists and literary figures. The statue (by Alajos Stróbl, 1893) in front of the museum entrance was erected to the memory of *János Arany,* the great epic poet.

In the big vestibule of the Museum with its three naves, we find the largest mosaic floor in Hungary which has remained intact from Roman times. From the vestibule we reach a dome-covered hall from which the two-armed ornamental staircase branches out. The ceiling is decorated with murals by Mór Than and Károly Lotz.

The exhibition on the first floor deals with *the history of the peoples who lived on Hungary's territory up to the Magyar Conquest.* Especially interesting are the remains of a palaeolithic settlement unearthed at Vértesszőlős in 1960. The rich collection of Bronze Age finds, of which a clay cart dating from 1800 B.C. is also worthy of mention, is followed by relics of Celtic culture: gold objects with oriental motifs, urns and burial vaults. Relics from the Roman period occupy three halls. Among the relics of industry and commerce are a reconstructed pottery workshop and the remains of a Roman villa. The objects of ancient Jewish and early Christian religious cults are also worth attention. From the burial places of the various tribes accompanying the Huns it is mainly jewels and horse gears that have been unearthed, but relics of German tribes, Avars and Franks, have also remained. From the so-called Great Moravian Empire of the Slavs, visitors can see the reconstructed model of a basilica.

The subject of the exhibition on the second floor is the *history of the Hungarian people from the Conquest of the country to 1849.* Early cemetery finds are followed by lovely Romanesque wood-carvings remaining from destroyed churches. A copy of the Hungarian royal crown from the eleventh and thirteenth centuries is exhibited in a separate showcase together with copies of the royal insignia. Glass cabinets hold coin finds and elaborate objects of medieval handicraft; the fourteenth-century ornamental fountain from King Matthias' Visegrád palace occupies a special place. The fine gold objects in the treasure-chamber came to the museum from the families of the aristocracy; in addition to a few early works of art they chiefly consist of ornamented objects in Baroque style, such as church relics and gilded weapons.

Relics of the fifteenth century, the period of Kings Sigismund and Matthias, are exhibited in a separate hall. The embroidered royal throne drapery, the ivory-ornamented saddle and the carved winged altar are not merely significant historical relics but works of art of a high standard, which bear witness of the advanced skills of the period. The oldest bookcase in Hungary and the stall from Nyírbátor, a fine inlaid work from Florence, belong to the early sixteenth century; the ceremonial habit of King Louis II, who fell in the field, and the contemporary portrait of Sultan Soliman II are reminders of the battle of Mohács (1526), which decided the country's fate. The tent of the Turkish commander with its oriental carpets is one of the museum's outstanding rarities. During the Turkish occupation, Transylvania remained an independent Hungarian principality; thus the ornamental weapons, ceremonial dresses, sepulchres and so on come from there. Relics of the Reformation date back to the same period. Furniture and weapons from the castles of Ferenc Rákóczi II, the leader of the eighteenth-century War of Independence, recall this period. The pillory and whipping-post illustrate the lot of the peasants. From the end of the century we find the gala suits and furniture of the nobility, as well as interior furnishings from Baroque and Rococo palaces. The period of enlightenment is illustrated by the decrees of Maria Theresa and Joseph II describing the duties of serfs, and also by rudimentary agricultural implements, relics of the peasant risings and of the history of the artisans' guilds. We can also see there the sword of the executioner of Buda which put an end to the lives of Ignác Martinovics and his seven companions, the leaders of the Hungarian republican movement. During the great national revival in the first half of the nineteenth century, manufactures developed fast, and the exhibition displays some of their tools. A large oil canvas depicts the laying of the foundation stone of the Chain Bridge—a fine part of the city skyline. Among the relics of the 1848–49 War of Independence we find the velvet chairs of the members of the Cabinet, and in the glass cases can be seen the uniforms of the National Army, as well as objects recalling the period's leading personalities. The tragic outcome of the War of Independence is recalled—in addi-

The vestibule of the National Museum

tion to other relics—by a woman's mourning dress from the 1850s.

The Hungarian royal crown and the royal insignia are exhibited in the great hall of the museum. The crown, dating from the eleventh and thirteenth centuries, the mantle from the eleventh century, as well as the sword, the sceptre and the orb are all valuable works of art which, after decades of vicissitudes—they were carried off by the escaping fascists—were ceremoniously returned from the United States in 1978.

The Museum of Applied Arts is situated at the intersection of Üllői út and the Great Boulevard, not far from the National Museum. Its majolica-covered roof, the façade with its Hindu-Islamic and Hungarian ceramics, and its interior with Turkish and Byzantine elements make it a characteristic example of the Hungarian Art Nouveau architecture of the turn of the century. Designed by Ödön Lechner, the foremost representative of this trend and Gyula Pártos, the building was constructed between 1893 and 1896.

The collections include:

Furniture: The most noteworthy pieces of the Hungarian exhibition are a Baroque pharmacy reconstructed in its original form, the library room, as well as coffered church ceilings painted with folk motifs. A rich collection of honeycake moulds and blue-dyers' blocks is also to be found here.

Ceramics and glass objects: This surveys the history of Hungarian ceramics and china. Its most precious pieces are the old products of the Zsolnay factory at Pécs and the Herend china factory, both established in the last century and still in existence, and the collection of stove-tiles. The glass collection contains several valuable art objects from the Antiquity and the Middle Ages.

Gold and silversmiths' works: The largest collection is the precious Esterházy treasure, with pieces from the fifteenth to eighteenth centuries, among them objects related to the person of King Matthias. A collection of jewels, clocks and watches, wrought-iron and ecclesiastical objects is also displayed here.

Textiles: Besides the relatively few objects of Hungarian origin, we find here a rich collection of Anatolian carpets, as well as masterpieces of sixteenth to eighteenth-century Flemish tapestry. Temporary exhibitions display old embroidered vestments and lacework. The most beautiful pieces of the historical costume collection have also come from the Esterházy family.

In addition to the rich collections mentioned above, other masterpieces of applied arts are also displayed at temporary exhibitions, such as ivory carvings, fancy leather goods, artistic book-bindings and objects made of various materials.

Walks to Suit Your Individual Interests

Three days in a city you have not visited before can be both too short and too long. Too short, because you can only see the best-known sights, the main historical parts of the city and the chief public collections. Yet it can also be too long, because the great number of new impressions and new sights can, by their very multitude, tire you out and make you long for a rest. We think that the walks we have described below will suit not only those who want to use the short time at their disposal to see things that particularly interest them personally, but also those who are tired of sightseeing and want a complete change and a chance to relax.

12

FOR LOVERS OF NATURE: THE BUDA HILLS

The right bank of the capital, Buda, is surrounded in a semicircle by the Buda hills, beginning and ending at the Danube. At one time they supplied stone, clay and timber for the construction of the city and vines grew on their slopes; now they offer city-dwellers pleasant walks and excursions and lovely views. The hillsides nearer to the river have already become garden suburbs, but not too far away one can still find slopes and ridges covered with forests and groves. In the Buda hills do not look for the overwhelming beauty of high mountains, or for the romantic remains of olden times. You will delight in the gentle slopes of what are hills, rather than mountains, and in the lush vegetation of elm or oak woods. You will be charmed, too, by the orchards and gardens of the sunny southern slopes. At any season of the year, if you take a stroll in the hills, with their invigorating air, you will find new enjoyment every time you go. In the spring, there are the snowdrops, the violets and the lilies of the valley, and the blossom of the fruit-trees is in full glory. In the summer, there is the wonderful fresh air after the stifling airlessness of the crowded city below. In the autumn, you will walk amidst the flaming colours of the trees on a soft carpet of fallen leaves. And in the winter, if there is enough snow—this depends on the weather, of course—you can ski and indulge in many other winter sports.

Buses and trams will take you from the town to the hills, and in the woods there are good motor roads and footpaths. There are three "mountain railways": the Cogwheel Railway up to Szabadság (Liberty) Hill, the Teleferic ("libegő") to the János Hill, and the Pioneers' Railway (Úttörővasút) which starts out from Hűvösvölgy and meanders through the picturesque countryside past János Hill as far as Széchenyi Hill. Footpaths are well marked and you may safely take any of them; everywhere you will find signs indicating direction, time and distance.

Hármashatár Hill and its neighbourhood. Frankel Leó út and Árpád fejedelem útja, two Buda streets parallel with the Danube leading northwards to Óbuda, take you to Kolosy tér near which, at the corner of Szépvölgyi út, the Baroque tower of Újlak Church rises above the little houses. The motor road of the 497-metre (1,515 ft.) Hármashatár Hill starts here. From the top you get a view all around the surrounding area: to the north there are the Pilis mountains, and at their foot the Danube reaching Budapest in two branches which pass on either side of Szentendre Island. Immediately below us lies Óbuda, with its big new housing estates sprouting up; further to the south we see the inner districts of the capital. To the west lies the other big group of the Buda hills with a lookout tower on János Hill, the highest point.

Szabadság (Liberty) Hill and its neighbourhood. The first villas of Budapest were built in this area in the early nineteenth century, among vineyards. Some of the houses still standing have neo-Classical façades and are protected as historical monuments; the charming simplicity of some of the old houses suggests Swiss influence. Starting out at Moszkva tér, we first pass *Városmajor,* a large park with lovely old trees, and reach the cylindrical *Hotel Budapest* and, opposite to it, the terminal of the *Cogwheel Railway*. This "mountain" railway built in 1874, with the Swiss Rigi railway as its model, was completely renewed in 1974–75. The line is 3,733 metres (4,106 yds.) long, with a rise in level of 315 metres (1,038 ft.). En route, looking down, we can enjoy the panorama of the garden suburbs of Budapest between Hármashatár Hill and Liberty Hill. The top terminal of the Cogwheel Railway is on Széchenyi Hill, near the Television Tower and the *Hotel Vörös Csillag*. Here we can board the *Pioneers' Railway,* or, after a 15 minutes' walk along the ridge between houses and gardens, we reach paths leading through fields and woods. On the hillside towards the city there are meadows and groves, on the other side denser woods. A ¾ hour's walk along the pleasant tourist path running through the wood alongside the motor road takes us to *János Hill.*

If you have chosen to take the 12-kilometre (7.5 m.) long ride on the narrow-gauge Pioneers' Railway, the train, winding through woods and valleys, will take you on around János Hill, through the Hűvösvölgy as far as the foot of the Hármashatár Hill where you will find a bus and tram terminal.

The János Hill can also be approached by the Teleferic ("libegő"). It starts at *No. 93* Zugligeti út, which can be reached from Moszkva tér by bus 158. The chairlifts of the 1.5-kilometre (about 1 mile) long cableway take you to the top station, from where the János Hill lookout is but a few minutes' walk. Should you want some variety in your tour, you can come back on the Pioneers' Railway which stops near by. János Hill is 529 metres (1,745 ft.) high, the lookout tower 23 metres (76 ft.); the latter was built by Frigyes Schulek, the designer of the Fishermen's Bastion, and from its top in clear weather there is a view of 70 to 80 kilometres (46–50 m.). Below the hill there is the largest unbroken wooded area of the Buda hills; to the west some parts of the Transdanubian mountains are visible; we get glimpses of the Danube here and there and the peaks of the Börzsöny mountains rise to the north. Beyond them is Czechoslovakia. At the foot of the hill lies Budakeszi út *(Hotel Európa)* which winds towards the northwest to forest-clad regions. To the east lies the Great Plain, with a few low hills in the region between the Danube and the river Tisza. The city centre is 6 to 8 kilometres (4–5 m.) away but its details are no longer discernible—only the towers, the tall white buildings of the new residential districts and the bridges will allow orientation. The trams and buses which take you to the city are only an hour's walk away; in addition, on Sundays and holidays there is a bus (J) which will take you straight from the lookout tower to the Inner City.

13

THE ZOOLOGICAL AND BOTANICAL GARDENS

The Zoological and Botanical Gardens of Budapest (see map 5) were opened on August 9, 1866, under the management of the famous scientist János Xantus. They then had 11 buildings with 500 animals. Between 1907 and 1912 they were reconstructed in their present form. In accordance with the romantic notions of that period, the individual animal houses imitate the architecture of exotic countries. During the Second World War three quarters of the buildings were destroyed and most of the animals and plants perished. Reconstruction and enlargement of the Zoo has been going on continuously since 1945; this is greatly limited by the fact that the Zoo, once located in the suburbs, is now, through the growth of the town, situated in the heart of the city and cannot be expanded any further. Together with the new, modern buildings, up-to-date methods for the rearing, breeding and upkeep of the animals were introduced. Today over 4,000 animals and about 10,000 botanical plants can be found in an area of 35 acres. Natural environments have been created for the animals; for instance, the polar bears, seals and bears live among artificial rocks, and animals from the steppes and the desert in large sanded areas. An interesting feature of the Zoo is that the hippopotamus pool is fed with thermal water, and this presumably is the reason why these animals multiply in captivity. Young mammals are placed in an "animal nursery" after weaning. The large palm house is rich in tropical plants of great variety, and the tropical, cold-water and sea-water aquariums and the terrarium are likewise abundantly supplied. The sea-water pools contain 70,000 litres (15,500 gallons) of salt water which are filtered twice daily. The small pond with its aquatic birds and the charming Japanese gardens are also worth a look.

FOR THOSE INTERESTED IN THE SUBTERRANEAN WORLD: THE CAVES

Budapest was built at the meeting place of two different geological regions. The Great Hungarian Plain extending to the bank of the Danube developed during the Quaternary period and the hard formations of the Buda hills date back to the Mesozoic era.

During the Quaternary and the Mesozoic eras, owing to mighty movements of the earth's crust, the country's present territory was repeatedly inundated by the ocean from the direction of what is today the Adriatic Sea. As a result, both the mountainous and flat regions of Budapest settled mainly on oceanic sediment. The surface, however, was formed by the prehistoric Danube: on the present-day Pest bank and in previous flood areas, it is composed of river sediment made up of Quaternary gravel, sand and silt deposits. The composition and mineral salt content of the thermal springs of Budapest are indications of the composition of the rocks which agglomerated in the long distant past.

Deep down in the Buda hills many caves are hidden. Most of them came into being on account of the hot springs or through water dissolving, and hollowing out, the rock. Some were formed by shifting inside the mountains, and finally some caves, of varying sizes, were dug out by man himself.

The most interesting caves are: the *János Molnár Spa Cave,* behind the warm-water Mill Pond (Malom-tó) in Frankel Leó utca, II, at the foot of Rose Hill (Rózsadomb) with water of a temperature of 25°C (77°F) in its snow-white stalagtite bottom. The *Szemlő Hill Cave* is one kilometre (0.6 m.) long and is covered with gypsum and stalactites. The *Pálvölgyi Cave,* with its 1,100-metre (0.8 m.) long walks and lovely stalactite formations, is also a most interesting sight. Nearby the *Mátyás Hill Cave,* likewise from the Eocene period, is hollowed out of limestone and marl and has a pond at its bottom fed by karstic water. The *Ferenc Hill Cave,* discovered beneath Törökvészi út in District II, is also a stalactite cave. In the neighbourhood of Hűvösvölgy we find the *Báthory* and *Hétlyuk Caves.*

At the foot of Gellért Hill, the sulphuric thermal spring feeding the Imre Baths has its source in the

Mátyás Hot-spring Cave in Tabán, and the *Mátyás, Árpád* and *Rákóczi springs* come from dolomite hollows on the eastern side of Gellért Hill.

Beneath Castle Hill, an immense *cave system* has developed in the limestone. Originally formed by the prehistoric Danube, the caves were further developed by men seeking shelter from enemy attacks, particularly because, owing to the water there, the enemy could not make them die of thirst. The caves could be reached through cellars in the houses above.

During quarrying for building materials, many artificial hollows and caves have been hollowed out in the limestone strata. The largest such caves on the Pest side are those of Kőbánya, and in Buda, the Budafok cellars. These are used for storing wine and beer, as well as for mushroom cultivation.

At present only the *Pálvölgyi Stalactite Cave* (162 Szépvölgyi út, II), *Szemlőhegyi Cave* (35 Pusztaszeri út, II) and a section of Buda's *Castle Cave* (No. 9 Úri utca, I) are open to visitors.

The other caves can only be visited by professionals with an official guide. For information contact the Hungarian Karst and Cave Exploring Association (Magyar Karszt és Barlangkutató Társulat) at No. 1–3 Anker köz, V; tel.: 217–293.

15

FOR THOSE INTERESTED IN THE HISTORY OF ARCHITECTURE: ANCIENT AND HISTORICAL MONUMENTS

Although the city was often ravaged by war, flood, and fire, an art-lover can still discover many beautiful and interesting architectural monuments in Budapest. In the Castle District of Buda, for instance, some of the medieval buildings still bear witness to the style of various periods. Baroque and neo-Classical material abounds; indeed, this latter style became almost characteristic of the national revival period. The residential parts of Pest, on the other hand, were built during the turn-of-the-century urbanization period, in a variety of eclectic styles.

The oldest settlement that existed on the territory of present-day Budapest dates back 2,000 years. In the

The Magdalene Tower and some gardens in the Castle District

first century A.D., when, after the Eraviscans, a Celtic tribe, Roman legions conquered Pannonia, the Western part of today's Hungary, their *limes* (border) became the Danube. The Roman legions founded Aquincum (see p. 64) at the site of the former Celtic Ak-ink.

From the **Roman period,** in addition to the ruins of Aquincum, many discoveries were made when new buildings started to be built on the area. The *Roman military public baths with a heating system* have been discovered almost intact: they can still be seen under the approach road to Árpád Bridge in Flórián tér, the supporting pillars and the heating area are well discern-

The Royal Palace: the Mace Tower

Rákóczi út with St. Roch's Chapel

ible beneath the floor. A uniquely beautiful find, discovered in the last decade, is the *mosaic floor,* now carefully protected (19–21 Meggyfa utca, III), which shows Heracles and Deianeira. The new thoroughfare alongside Aquincum runs next to the arcaded columns of the former aqueduct.

The Mongolian invasion of 1241–42 almost totally destroyed the country; as a result, the remains of the constructions and churches which the kings of the House of Árpád had built **after the Conquest of the country** can only be found in some foundation walls buried deep in the ground. Following the withdrawal of the Mongols, King Béla IV started to rebuild the coun-

101

try: he had fortresses built and towns surrounded by stone walls. This was the time when the town of Buda began to take shape.

For this reason, the capital is not very rich in **Romanesque monuments;** nevertheless it is worth visiting the *ruins of the Premonstratensian chapel* on Margaret Island (between the Grand Hotel and the open-air theatre), and the foundation wall of the southern tower of the *Inner City Parish Church* (Március 15. tér, V.).

The birthplace of Ignác Semmelweis (now the Museum of Medical History) in the Tabán district

The courtyard of the Pest County Hall in the Inner City

Gothic monuments are mainly to be found in the Castle District (see map 1); first among them are the ruins of the old *Royal Palace* and *Chapel* as well as the Gothic statues discovered a few years ago, and the fortifications (Castle Museum, see p. 38); the *Church of Our Lady* (Matthias Church), though with neo-Gothic details, still recalls the original architectural trends of the thirteenth and fourteenth centuries in its ground plan and strong plastic effect. The walls of the Gothic tower of the *Magdalene Church* (Kapisztrán tér, I) have also survived. The walls of the Dominican *St. Nicholas' Church* (Hess András tér, I) also date back to the Middle Ages; its buttressed chancel forms a section of the eastern ramparts. Several lovely Gothic *houses* in the Castle District have also survived, as well as typical niches with seats in the doorways.

The first illustration of Buda is contained in the *Schedel Chronicle* of 1490. For centuries it was thought that the picture showing a Gothic city with many steeples was an idealized one, and only the excavations after 1945 confirmed the fact that Buda was once indeed the country's largest and most beautiful Gothic city. The Gothic relics in the Inner City Parish Church are equally precious, and on Margaret Island the ruins of the Gothic convent of the Dominican nuns are also worth seeing.

Renaissance monuments are now mainly displayed in the Castle Museum. Of these, the sixteenth-century Italian-type fortifications of the northeast ramparts of Buda are of particular interest; the best illustration of these is the *Southern Round Bastion* near the entrance to the Castle Museum. Two Renaissance tabernacles can be found in the Inner City Parish Church. An *excursion to Visegrád* (see p. 130) will offer a richer choice of Renaissance monuments.

Of the examples of **Turkish architecture,** it is especially worthwhile seeing the *Rudas Baths* (Gellért rakpart, I), and the domed hall of the *Király Baths* (82–86 Fő utca, II; the ramparts of Buda, the western wall, fortified with circular battlements and towers (Tóth Árpád sétány, I), and, last but not least, the *türbe (tomb) of Gül Baba,* who has become a legendary figure of the Turkish occupation (14 Mecset utca, II).

After the Turks were driven out of the country, the new buildings were erected in the **Baroque style;** this new, fashionable European style was introduced by the foreign settlers and religious orders called in to repopulate Buda. Palaces were built by the aristocracy, churches and monasteries erected, and at Maria Theresa's decree, the rebuilding of the Royal Palace was started. Hence, Budapest is rich in Baroque historical monuments; however, these are to be found scattered in various parts of the city rather than in one particular

The central synagogue in Dohány utca

area. The most important monuments of this period are the southern, so-called Maria Theresa wing of the new *Royal Palace,* the former *Town Hall of Buda* (2 Szentháromság utca, I), and several particularly beautiful mansions in the Castle District, such as the buildings at

Nos. 1,7 and *23 Táncsics utca* and at *No. 3 Dísz tér.* Outstandingly beautiful examples of secular Baroque architecture are the former Invalids' House, now the *Budapest Town Hall* (9–11 Városház utca, V), the former Péterffy Palace, today the *"Százéves"* (Hundred-year-old) *restaurant* (2 Pesti Barnabás utca, V), and the one-time Rudnyánszky Castle, which is now the *Nagytétény Castle Museum* (Nagytétény, XXII). Some of the loveliest Baroque ecclesiastical buildings are: in Buda, *St. Anne's Church and Rectory* (Batthyány tér, I) with the former *St. Elizabeth's Convent and Church* nearby, and the *Parish Church of Óbuda* (Óbudai utca, III); in Pest the *Inner City Parish Church* (Március 15. tér, V), the *University Church* and, adjoining it, the seminary building originally erected as a *monastery of the Paulite friars,* the library of which is one of the most beautiful Baroque interiors of Budapest (Egyetem tér, V), the old *Franciscan Church* (2 Károlyi Mihály utca, V) and *St. Roch's Chapel* (31 Rákóczi út, VIII).

At the beginning of the nineteenth century, well-to-do citizens had their houses decorated in the *style of Louis XVI*—the so-called **"zopf" style.** It is worth looking at the *group of houses at Nos. 5, 6* and *7 Bécsikapu tér, I,* the former *White Cross* (Fehér Kereszt) *Inn* (Batthyány tér, I), the *birthplace of Ignác Semmelweis* which today houses the *Museum of Medical History* (1–3 Apród utca, I); and on the Pest side, the *Hungarian Orthodox Church* (Petőfi tér, V), the façade of which was reconstructed by Miklós Ybl, and the *Serbian Orthodox Church* (66 Váci utca, V).

Of the **neo-Classical** buildings typical of the architecture of the beginning of the nineteenth century, we list here only a few characteristic ones: the *Hungarian National Museum* (14–16 Múzeum körút, VIII), the structure of the *Chain Bridge pillars,* the entrance to the *Castle Hill Tunnel,* the *Lukács Baths* (25–29 Frankel Leó utca, II), the *Lutheran Church* at Deák tér, the *Calvinist Church* on Kálvin tér; further, the former *Károlyi Palace,* now the *Petőfi Literary Museum* (16 Károlyi Mihály utca, V), the *Pest County Hall* (7 Városház utca, V) and numerous *blocks of flats* in the Inner City, such as the buildings at *Nos. 1* and *3* Akadémia utca, and other houses in the Arany János, Dorottya, József Attila and Ferenczy István utca. It is also worthwhile seeing the former *Óbuda Synagogue* (163 Lajos utca, III); it is interesting to note that while

The Városmajor Church

the majority of synagogues are built in Moorish style, this one is, exceptionally, a neo-Classical building. It now houses a studio of the Hungarian Television.

The buildings which characterize the present look of the inner parts of the city were built in the **historical-eclectic style of the end of the nineteenth century,** mainly for the Millennium, which was celebrated with dazzling pomp. Some fine specimens are the *main* building of the Royal Palace and its wing facing *Christina Town*, the *Fishermen's Bastion*, the *Parliament House*, the *Vigadó Concert Hall* (Vigadó tér, V), the former Supreme Court building now housing the *Ethnographical Museum*, the *Opera House*, the *Basilica*, *Hősök tere* and its monuments and buildings and the *Vajdahunyad Castle* complex (Széchenyi Island, City Park, XIV). The mansions of the aristocracy in the quarter behind the National Museum present the harmonious effect characteristic of the period's architecture; on the other hand, the architectural ornaments imitative of historical styles on many of the blocks of flats are out of place.

Some architects tried to create a characteristically Hungarian style by introducing Hungarian peasant motifs; for ornamental motifs they drew on Hungarian folk art and for building elements on Islamic architecture in India; the houses were covered with pyrogranite and majolica from the Zsolnay factory. The most prominent representative of this romantic school was Ödön Lechner; the former *Hungarian Foreign Trade Bank*, now the National Bank of Hungary (4 Rosenberg házaspár utca, V), the *Museum of Applied Arts* (33–37 Üllői út, IX), the *Institute of Geology* (14 Népstadion út, XIV), the *Synagogue* in Dohány utca were designed by him and Gyula Pártos.

All schools of **modern architecture** have left a mark on the developing capital. Between the two world wars, the new building materials—reinforced concrete and glass—became typical of the construction of the garden estates of Buda and the housing estates to the north of the Parliament. In the inner parts of the city some public buildings from this period without any special characteristic style are: the present-day *Budapest Police Headquarters* (16–18 Deák Ferenc utca, V), the *Városmajor Church* (Csaba utca, XII), the so-called "Rózsavölgyi House" at 5 Martinelli tér, V.

In fact it was only in the years of reconstruction, from the 1950s on, that big new architectural units were built which again lent character to the city. The blocks of the new housing estates (the Lágymányos and the József Attila estates) are separated by strips of parkland which permit the residents to enjoy the sunshine and air. Individual planning has since the end of the 1960s been more and more replaced by blocks of flats built of prefabricated elements (Óbuda, Kelenföld, Újpalota, Békásmegyer housing estates). Lively debates charac-

New housing estate at the Pest end of Árpád Bridge

terize the planning of public and office buildings; in this manner have arisen such state offices, research institutes, office buildings or hotels as, for instance, the *People's Stadium* (3–5 Istvánmezei út, XIV), the *Hotel Budapest* (47 Szilágyi Erzsébet fasor, II), *the Hotel Duna Inter-Continental* (4 Apáczai Csere János utca, V), the *Hotel Forum* (12 Apáczai Csere János utca, V) and the *Hotel Atrium-Hyatt* (2 Roosevelt tér, V), the *Hotel Thermal* (Margaret Island), the *Health Sanatorium of Trade Unions* (on Rose Hill), the *Hotel Budapest Hilton* (Hess András tér, I) the *Southern Railway Station* (Alkotás utca, I), the *Budapest Sports Hall* (48–52 Hungária körút, XIV), the *Hotel Novotel* with the *Budapest Convention Centre* (1–3 Jagelló út, XII) standing next to it, and many other public buildings.

16

FOR THOSE WHO LIKE FINE ARTS AND ETHNOGRAPHY

The majority of paintings are in two big collections: the *Museum of Fine Arts* (see p. 72) and the *Hungarian National Gallery*. Wall paintings and statues, of course, also decorate the churches as well as old and new buildings. For instance, the choir of the Inner City Parish Church still contains some remnants of fifteenth-century wall paintings (see p. 44). The altar-pieces and frescoes of Baroque churches were painted mainly by Austrian and Hungarian masters under Italian influence, the public buildings (Parliament, Opera House, National Museum, Basilica, etc.) and the large blocks of flats of the eclectic period abound in the sgraffiti and frescoes of the academic schools.

Some of the works of sculpture stand in public squares, but no medieval works of art can be found among them; these are only in museums. The group of fourteenth-century statues and fragments excavated in the Royal Palace in 1974 is of special interest. They are displayed in the Budapest History Museum. The Baroque period, too, is represented by some religious statues. Dating from the last century, however, there are many fountains and other monuments. In the Inner City district statues of historical personages in an academic style predominate.

Even after 1945, a dignified style prevailed in the plastic arts (for instance, the Liberation Monument on Gellért Hill, the Dózsa statue in Tabán and the statue of Kossuth in front of the Parliament). The more recent schools, which do not aim at meticulously perfected details, but wish to impress with their striking general composition, have produced such achievements as the Marx–Engels statue (near Margaret Bridge, the work of György Segesdy), the statue of Lenin (by Pál Pátzay) and the Monument of the Hungarian Soviet Republic (by István Kiss, in Dózsa György út), as well as the ornamental figures and fountains of the parks and the new housing estates.

The **Hungarian National Gallery** (in the building of the Royal Palace, wings B-C-D) presents outstanding works of Hungarian painting and sculpture. Periodical exhibitions are run in special halls.

The staircase landings are adorned with *nineteenth*

Kossuth Lajos tér: the building of the Ethnographical Museum as seen from the Parliament

and *twentieth-century statues*. *István Ferenczy* (1792–1856) is an outstanding representative of Hungarian sculpture; a few of his portraits of classical simplicity are on show there. *Miklós Izsó* (1831–1875) is represented with figures of dancing peasants which clearly demonstrate the originality of his talent. *Ferenc Medgyessy* (1881–1958) is the great sculptor of this century. The other modern statues present various aspirations of realistic delineation.

As regards *nineteenth-century* painting, only the greatest masterpieces from an extremely rich collection can be seen at the permanent exhibition for the time being. *Mihály Munkácsy* (1844–1900), who worked in Paris, is characterized by powerfully realistic compositions depicted in dark tones. *Pál Szinyei Merse* (1845–1900) and *László Mednyánszky* (1825–1919) are two outstanding representatives of *plein-air* painting.

The various schools of the *fin-de-siècle* are typically reflected in the paintings of *Károly Kernstok* (1873–1940) and *József Rippl-Rónai* (1861–1927).

The great exhibition of *Baroque painting* largely comprises pieces from palaces and ecclesiastical institutions. Best known among these are the paintings of *Ádám Mányoki* (1673–1757), especially his self-portrait and his portrait of Prince Ferenc Rákóczi II. In addition, there are the fertile *Biedermeier* landscape and portrait painters: *Károly Markó, Károly Brocky* and *Miklós Barabás*.

On the second floor can be seen paintings by the masters of the so-called *Nagybánya School,* who revived twentieth-century Hungarian painting. Turning away from the Arcadian, *Simon Hollósy* (1857–1918), *Károly Ferenczy* (1862–1917) and *János Thorma* (1870–1937) strove to establish a national style of painting.

Located on the ground floor are the collections of medieval stonework finds, late Gothic winged altars, Gothic wooden statues and fourteenth-century panel paintings, while up in the vaulted hall visitors can see *a medal and graphics exhibition.* Periodical exhibitions of *contemporary artists* are always very interesting.

The Ethnographical Museum

On the eastern side of Kossuth Lajos tér stands the Ethnographical Museum, a building of neo-Baroque character decorated with Renaissance elements. It was built between 1893 and 1896 to the plans of Alajos Hauszmann, to house the Supreme Court. The group of statues on the tympanum (by György Zala, 1858–1937) depict a court hearing; above the façade the antique chariot drawn by three horses symbolizes the victory of justice, the two male figures (by János Fadrusz, 1858–1903) on both sides represent legislators, and the statues ornamenting the cornice portray various figures dispensing justice.

The building is 125 metres (137 yds.) long. From its main entrance we reach the 40 metre (44 yds.) long and 24 metre (26 yds.) wide hall decorated with marble and gilding, and the ceremonial staircase. The hall is decorated with a fresco by Károly Lotz: in the centre is Justitia, the goddess of justice, holding the sword and scales in her hand; she is surrounded by law-abiding citizens, offenders and groups personifying various professions.

The exhibitions of the Ethnographical Museum: on

The Nagytétény Castle Museum

the first floor, the life-style, culture and art of the Hungarian peasantry; the relics of the peasants' work, agriculture, animal breeding, various trades and handicrafts are followed by the mementoes of holidays and of Hungarian folk art. On the second floor is an exhibition of selected examples of the development of the major phases of various societies from Asia, Africa, the South Sea Islands, Indonesia, Australia and America. The material from the Siberian Finno-Ugrian tribes related to Hungarians has been collected by Antal Reguly and János Jankó, among others; the collection of old artifacts from early New Guinea (Lajos Biró and Sámuel Fenichel), from East Africa (Sámuel Teleki) and from Central Africa (Emil Torday) are also on display here.

The **Kiscell Museum** (108 Kiscelli utca, III) is in itself of interest as a historical monument; erected in the mid-eighteenth century as a Trinitarian monastery, it later served as military barracks and then as a hospital. In 1912 it became the property of Miksa Schmidt, a cabinet-maker, who added to it the Louis-XVI-style portals of the Vienna Ministry of War which he had also bought, and also moved his collections here. Between 1929 and 1943 the building—by then the property of the capital—became part of the Budapest Museum; today it houses the Museum's modern material. We mention it here, because it also has a significant collection of works by twentieth-century Hungarian painters.

The **Nagytétény Castle Museum** (9 Csókási Pál utca, Nagytétény, XXII) is located in one of the capital's suburbs in the southern part of Buda. Following its post-war restoration, this two-storey Baroque building (by András Mayerhoffer, 1743–51) has become a museum. Its walls are covered by wall paintings from the eighteenth and nineteenth centuries, discovered during the restoration works; the Gothic walls of one of the reconstructed timbered roof halls also came to light that time. In its halls we can see exhibitions of artistic furniture and interiors: "European furniture in the fifteenth and sixteenth centuries", "Hungarian cabinet-making in the sixteenth century" and "Nineteenth-century artistic Hungarian furniture". (The Museum can be reached from Móricz Zsigmond körtér by tram 47 or bus 3.)

BUDAPEST FOR MUSIC-LOVERS

At the turn of the century the music life of the capital started to thrive, and later, through the art of *Béla Bartók* (1881–1945) and *Zoltán Kodály* (1882–1967), it burst into the international world of music and is today an integral and recognized part of it. Hungarian artists and ensembles—including non-professional groups which have attained a high artistic level during the past two decades—are welcome guests in the concert halls of foreign countries, and the most famous artists from abroad likewise welcome an invitation to perform in Hungary. Since the official concert agency itself organizes over 2,000 classical music concerts it is evident that music-lovers will find active music life at all seasons of the year.

The concerts and first-night performances of the Budapest Musical Weeks, which are held every year, are followed with great interest the world over, as are the Musical Competitions, a contest held every three years for young performers; similarly great interest has been expressed in the various music festivals, the folk-music and folk-dance programmes, and also in the performances of amateur choruses, orchestras and dance ensembles.

The most outstanding *concerts* in the capital are held in the Erkel Theatre and in the big and small concert halls of the Liszt Ferenc Academy of Music, the Budapest Convention Centre, in the concert room of the Vigadó and in the Church of Our Lady (Matthias Church); during the summer, concerts of high standard are given in the so-called "Music Court" on Castle Hill (62 Úri utca, I), in the aisle of the chapel renovated as part of the Hilton Hotel, and in the park of the Zichy Castle in Óbuda. Opera and ballet performances are held in the Margaret Island Open-Air Theatre, and musical comedies are on the programmes of the open-air theatre in the Városmajor Park (District XII) and another in southern Buda known as the Budai Parkszínpad (District XI).

Musical life has been enriched by regularly held concerts in the Hungarian National Gallery and the main auditorium of the Hungarian Academy of Sciences (28–30, Országház utca, I).

The largest symphonic orchestras are the *State Con-*

cert Orchestra, the *Orchestra of the Budapest Philharmonic Society,* the *Hungarian Radio and Television Orchestra* and the *Budapest Festival Orchestra,* which, with their excellent conductors—and together with Hungarian and foreign soloists of international fame and first-class choruses—have greatly enhanced the good name of Hungarian music both abroad and at home.

The musical life of the capital is similarly enriched by excellent chamber-music ensembles, which also receive many invitations from abroad; to mention a few: the Bartók String Quartet, the Kodály String Quartet, the Ferenc Liszt Chamber Music Orchestra, the Budapest Chamber Music Ensemble and the Budapest Wind Instrument Quintet.

The Opera House, the shrine of Hungarian and international opera since 1884, together with the *Erkel Theatre,* its associate theatre opened in 1953, has an impressively large selection of operas in its repertoire. Furthermore it has presented many Hungarian musical compositions which have started out on the road to world fame from there. The chief of these are: "Prince Bluebeard's Castle", "The Wooden Prince" and "The Miraculous Mandarin" by Béla Bartók; "The Spinning Room" and "János Háry" by Zoltán Kodály; Poldini's "Carnival Wedding"; "King Pomade's New Dress" and "The Tragedy of Man" by György Ránki; Emil Petrovics's "C'est la guerre" and "Crime and Punishment"; "Blood Wedding" and "Hamlet" by Sándor Szokolay; "Zsigmond Báthori" by Zoltán Horusitzky and "Csongor and Tünde" by Attila Bozay. Today the world knows not only the names of such Hungarian composers as Ferenc Liszt (1811–1886), Ferenc Erkel (1816–1893), Béla Bartók and Zoltán Kodály, but also those of several members of the youngest generation, such as György Kurtág, Zsolt Durkó, Attila Bozay, Sándor Balassa and many others.

The *Hungarian State Folk Ensemble,* formed in 1950, strives to present Hungarian folk music and dancing and choral art at a high artistic level, and has made several guest appearances outside the country. It has inspired other groups to revive Hungarian folklore, folk tales and customs, songs and dances, and to present them in an artistic manner. As a result, today many professional or amateur groups delight the visitors every night at the Folklore Centre (47 Fehérvári út, XI) and on other stages with their authentic presentation of

Hungarian folklore, which still has something to say to modern man.

The *Municipal Operetta Theatre* (17 Nagymező utca, VI) continues to present with great success the already classical works of Hungarian and foreign composers and also modern musicals. We mention in particular the names of Pál Ábrahám, Mihály Eisemann, Szabolcs Fényes, Jenő Huszka, Victor Jacobi, Imre Kálmán, Ferenc Lehár, Hervé, Franz Suppé, Jacques Offenbach, Johann Strauss.

There is indeed a very wide choice for lovers of light entertainment: dance music is broadcast by the radio and television and in clubs, popular theatres and "youth parks".

In restaurants you mainly hear gipsy music. The gipsy bands play not only authentic Hungarian and gipsy folk music, but also pseudo-Hungarian songs from the last century and the turn of the century; in addition they entertain their guests with operetta *potpourri* and drawing-room pieces. In their orchestras, in addition to stringed instruments we find a clarinet, or a Hungarian clarinet *(tárogató)* and a cymbalum (*cimbalom,* a stringed instrument played with hammers). They play without a score and improvise as the mood takes them; guests often join in.

18

BUDAPEST, THE CITY OF BATHS

In one respect Budapest is unique: it is at one and the same time a famous spa and a great city. It is ideal for rest and relaxation, with an abundance of medicinal waters almost unequalled in Europe; yet it is able to offer this rest and relaxation in the framework of a sparkling and busy metropolis.

Even 2,000 years ago, the settlement here was called in Celtic Ak-ink, meaning "abundant water". Hence the Roman name Aquincum to designate their town whose aqueducts were fed by thermal springs. In the Middle Ages hospitals were established near the medicinal springs. The Turks used the spas for their religious purification. Modern hydropathic therapy began in the early nineteenth century. Budapest is still very rich in medicinal spas. Most of them are springs or artesian wells rising up from great depths with a high content of

The inner court of the Császár Baths

dissolved radioactive salts of considerable curative power. 70 million litres (about 16 million gallons) of medicinal water stream out daily from 117 thermal springs on both sides of the Danube and on Margaret Island. These medicinal waters contain a high degree of calcium, magnesium, hydrocarbonate, sulphate ions and hydrogen sulphide, and the springs at Gellért Hill have, in addition, highly effective radioactive properties. The medicinal waters of Budapest are used mainly for the treatment of rheumatic diseases, female ailments, different degrees of nervous exhaustion and metabolic disturbances, but the thermal water of the springs also fills the open-air baths and the mineral-water bottles.

For information about medicinal baths apply to the Municipal Baths Centre (Fővárosi Fürdőigazgatóság, 25 Guszev utca, V).

Medicinal Baths

Gellért Medicinal Baths, 4 Kelenhegyi út, XI (at the Buda end of Liberty Bridge)

Fed by 13 springs of 27–48°C (82–118°F). Thermal steam baths, hot-air and steam chambers, thermal tub-baths, aerated water and salt baths. Treatments: mud packs, massages, physical and electrotherapy, traction baths, etc. Recommended for the treatment of diseases of the joints, rheumatism, neuralgia, inflammations, and post-paralysis treatment. Also for metabolic disturbances and diseases of the respiratory tract. Pools: in summer *open-air pool* with artificial waves, in winter indoor bubble baths.

Lukács Medicinal Baths, 25–29 Frankel Leó utca, II

Fed by 17 springs, the temperature of the water is 17–50°C (60–122°F). Thermal steam baths, hot-air and steam chambers, thermal tub-baths, aerated and salt baths, mud packs. The beautiful and still intact Turkish pool of the *Császár baths* nearby (at No. 31–33) is also worth seeing. Drinking-cures. Recommended for the treatment of rheumatism, arthritis, inflammation, muscular and neuralgic diseases. The *open-air swimming pools* of the Lukács baths are open to the public both in winter and summer. Next to it we find the National Rheumatological and Physicotherapeutics Institute (Országos Reuma és Fizikoterápiai Intézet), which can accommodate a thousand patients, and on the hillside above, the Trade Union sanatorium.

Király Baths, 84 Fő utca, II

Fed by the springs of the Lukács baths. Thermal tub and steam baths. The beautiful pool, dating from the Turkish occupation, is worth seeing.

Rác (Imre) Baths, 8 Hadnagy utca, I (at the Buda end of Elizabeth Bridge, in the Tabán park)

Thermal steam baths, hot-air and steam chambers, thermal tub-baths. Pool dating from the Turkish occupation. Recommended for the treatment of arthritis, muscular and neuralgic pains.

Rudas Medicinal Baths, 9 Döbrentei tér, I (at the Buda end of Elizabeth Bridge, on the Buda Danube bank)

Fed by 8 springs, the temperature of the water is 42°C (108°F). Thermal steam baths, hot-air and steam chambers, radioactive tub-baths. Recommended for the treatment of arthritis, muscular and neuralgic pains, physical and mental exhaustion. Drinking the water of the "Juventus" and "Hungária" springs is often effective in gastric conditions, internal disorders and catarrhal defects of the respiratory organs. It is an ancient bath dating from the Turkish period. The *indoor swimming pool* is open in winter and summer.

Széchenyi Medicinal Baths, 11 Állatkerti körút, City Park, XIV

From 1,250 m (4100 ft.) deep artesian wells 4,500 litres (1,000 gallons) of water of 70°C (150°F) gush forth each minute. Thermal steam baths, hot-air and steam chambers, thermal tub-baths, aerated and salt baths, hydropathic cures, mud packs, massages, physical and electrotherapy, drinking cures. Recommended for the treatment of rheumatism, arthritis, muscular and neuralgic diseases, and for the follow-up treatment of injuries, poliomyelitis and fractures. The *open-air pools*—with a separate pool for children—are open both in winter and summer.

Swimming pools and open-air baths

Alfréd Hajós Sports Swimming Pool, Margaret Island

This was built in 1930–31 to the designs of the architect Alfréd Hajós, winner of two gold medals at the 1896 Athens Olympic Games. Next to the Olympic-sized pool it also has a pool for diving and high-diving; the names of Hungarian swimmers and water-polo players who have been champions at the Olympic Games are engraved on marble tablets on the wall of the hall. International and national championships and water-polo matches are held in front of the grandstand seating 6,000 spectators. The 33.5 m (37 yds.) indoor pool, as well as the 50 m (55 yds.) and 33.5 m (37 yds.) outdoor pools are open to the general public at stated hours of the day, both in winter and summer. Both outdoors and indoors, there are separate pools for children.

Béla Komjádi Sports Swimming Pool (at the old Császár Baths, 2–4, Komjádi Béla utca, II)

A modern Olympic-sized pool in a hall with a sliding roof which is opened in summer.

Palatinus Open-Air Baths, Margaret Island

The pools are filled with artesian water of a temperature of 38–42°C (102–108°F). Its lawns and gardens can accommodate 30,000 bathers. There are a 120 metre (132 yds.) long pool, a pool with artificial waves, a cold-water pool with a fountain and a pool with hot thermal water.

Római-part Open-Air Baths (Római-parti erdei strandfürdő), Rozgonyi Piroska utca, III (at the station of the suburban express railway)

The Turkish pool of the Rudas Baths

Next to it is the Motel Venus with a restaurant and an international first-class camping site.

Szabadság Open-Air Baths, Dagály utca, XIII (at the Pest end of Árpád Bridge)
The 50-metre (55 yds.) long swimming pool and the thermal-water pools are filled by the "Béke" spring with a temperature of 42°C (108°F). Open in winter and summer.

Csillaghegy Árpád Open-Air Baths, 3 Pusztakúti út, III (It can be reached by the suburban express railway starting at Batthyány tér)

The two pools of different temperatures and the special children's pool are set in a large park. You will find a tourist hostel, a motel and a restaurant nearby.

Pünkösdfürdő Open-Air Swimming Pool, 272 Vörös Hadsereg útja, III (The direct approach is by the river boat service from the Danube, or by bus from Óbuda)

A 50-metre (55 yds.) long swimming pool and a children's pool are set in a lovely large park.

19

FOR SPORTS LOVERS

Hungarians are very fond of sports. As early as the beginning of the century Hungarian sport was outstanding by international standards, and since 1945 it has become even more distinguished. The secret of its success lies in the highly-organized character of Hungarian sports carried on in factories and schools. New talents keep arising, so there are great numbers of qualified sportsmen on all levels. The most outstanding results have been achieved in ball games, fencing, modern pentathlon, boxing, wrestling and weightlifting, and naturally these sports attract the greatest number of spectators. 112 Olympic gold medals and countless world and European titles and records bear witness to the achievements of Hungarian sportsmen.

Budapest is the centre of the country's sporting life. Here are the best-known sports clubs, several of which can boast a brilliant past; all have their own sports grounds and buildings. And here fans will find sporting events worth seeing at any season of the year.

The most important sports ground is the *People's Stadium* (Népstadion). According to foreign visitors and sports journalists this is one of the most beautiful and best equipped stadiums in Europe. The grandstand is supported by 18 open-work reinforced concrete pylons. There are 73,200 numbered seats. Evening events can be held on the splendid soft grass and on the cinder and artificial tracks, for 15,000 electric bulbs provide almost daytime lighting. The electric scoreboard is a Hungarian patent which has served as a model for similar ones in several great sports establishments in different parts of the world. Opened in 1982, the *Budapest Sports Hall* (52 Hungária körút, XIV) is Budapest's largest indoor sports centre. It is suitable for every kind of indoor competition and has a maximum seating capacity of 12,500.

Next to the People's Stadium, in the neighbourhood of the Eastern Railway Station, we find some smaller sports grounds: the *Little Stadium* (Kisstadion), the indoor *National Sports Hall* (Sportcsarnok) and *Games Hall* (Játékcsarnok), and the *Millenary Sports Ground* (Millenáris Sportpálya) used for cycling races. Ice-hockey matches and figure-skating competitions are held on the *City Park Artificial Skating Rink* (Városligeti Műjégpálya; Népstadion út, XIV) and in the Little Stadium. The *National Sports Swimming Pool* on Margaret Island is the scene of swimming, diving and water-polo events. In its indoor and outdoor pools the Olympic champion Hungarian swimmers and water-polo players have trained; it has seen many world records and world and European championships. The other great centre of swimming is the pool of the *Budapest Railwaymen's Sports Club* (Budapesti Vasutas Sport Club—BVSC; 2 Szőnyi út, XIV). There is an outdoor *Tennis Stadium* on Margaret Island; an indoor one in the *Vasas Sport Club* (11–13 Pasaréti út, II).

The most popular sport—one could call it the national sport—is football. The National League consists of autumn and spring rounds; in the summer various cups are competed for, the most outstanding one being the Hungarian People's Republic Cup—the final matches of this are played in the summer. Matches are played in the People's Stadium and on the different clubs' football grounds. The most important clubs are:

Csepel Sports Club (1 Béke tér, XXI) 12,000 seats;

FTC (129 Üllői út, IX) 35,000 seats;

Honvéd Sports Club (1–3 Temető utca, XIX) 10,000 seats;

MTK (6 Hungária körút, VIII) 35,000 seats;

Újpesti Dózsa Sports Club (13 Megyeri út, IV) 31,000 seats;

Vasas Sports Club (58 Fáy utca, XIII) 17,000 seats.

If, as a change from all your sightseeing, you would like to take part yourself in some sporting activity, we would particularly recommend swimming or hiking. On page 151 you will find a list of swimming pools and open-air baths, and on page 93 the most picturesque walks for tourists in the Buda hills. There are, of course, many other possibilities for shorter or longer walks and excursions; hikers' maps and tourist associations will give you further guidance.

Open-air gymnasiums in the woods of Liberty Hill, on Margaret Island and in Hűvösvölgy are at the disposal of sedentary workers and of all those who need some physical exercise now and again. Why don't *you* have a go?

Though not active sport, *horse races* provide pleasant entertainment. Galloping races are organized from spring to autumn with excellent Hungarian and foreign horses at the *Galloping Race Course* (Lóversenypálya; 2 Dobi István út, X; at the Pillangó utca station of the Metro). The *Trotting Race Course* (Ügetőverseny-Pálya; 9 Kerepesi út, VIII; at the Keleti Metro station) is open all the year round. At both race courses you can back your fancy.

20

PLACES OF TECHNOLOGICAL INTEREST

Hungary is one of those European countries where modern technical development began rather late, in the mid-nineteenth century, and where we find almost no relics from the heroic age of iron, steel, steam and electricity. In the second half of the century, however, the Hungarian capital began quickly to make up for lost time. It became the country's foremost industrial city, with thoroughfares and public utilities built in conformity with the high level of the time.

The *Chain Bridge* was completed after fifteen years' work in the middle of the century, in 1849. István Széchenyi, the great Hungarian politician who organized the construction work of the bridge, had to fight energetically for the realization of his plan. Besides political and economic arguments, he had to overcome the most varied technical objections, for instance, that the width of the Danube could not be spanned, that the mud in the river-bed could not support the pillars, that the pillars would be carried away by drifting ice in the winter, or that they would obstruct the ice and would cause floods, and so on. However, the British engineer William Tierny Clark was able to take into account the natural potentialities and he designed

The Danube bank in Buda

a bridge suspended on chains which were anchored to underground chain-lockers. The technical solution of the present, reconstructed bridge is similar to that of the original one, the pillars and the chain-lockers are the same, too. However, the structure of the bridge is more modern. The chains and the bridge-deck were first replaced by stronger ones in the 1900s. In January 1945 the bridge was blown up by the Germans, but in 1949 it was rebuilt. This prominent and beautiful technical achievement is today one of the symbols of Budapest.

The *embankments* were built between the 1870s and the 1900s during the regulation of the Danube. A concrete foundation of about 1.50 metres (about 5 ft.) was placed on steel beams and over this was built the hard limestone river wall. The area behind the wall was then filled in to form the quays. Large ships lay directly alongside the quays themselves; for smaller vessels flights of steps running to the level of the water were built at certain points. As a third variant slopes without steps were built. The upper wall rises 3 to 4 m (10 to 13 ft.) above the lower quay, and reaches the level of the streets. Its parapets protect the capital against a rise of level of 10 metres (33 ft.). Up to the 1930s the quays witnessed a busy trade life: agricultural products, building materials, fuel and package cargoes were unloaded here. Since then loading has been carried out in closed harbours and the 12-kilometre (7.5 m.) long embankments have become motor roads and at the same time impressive technological relics of nineteenth-century engineering.

Still functioning, and all the more for that an interesting technical relic, is the old *Underground Railway* now also called Metro Line 1 (renewed in 1973), which takes us to the City Park. To distinguish it from its younger brother, the deep-running Metro, the inhabitants of Budapest call it the "Little Underground". The 3-km (2 m.) long line was completed in 1896, the millennium of the Magyar Conquest. It is a so-called "cut-and-cover" railway, meaning that during its construction the roadway was broken up, a ditch was dug and then covered with iron girders. The clearance of the track is small, the suspension of the cars is at the height of the axles and the wheels have been placed under the elevated drivers' cabins. The stations are covered with tiles, and the iron structures are decorated in the Art Nouveau style, which conjures up the atmosphere of the turn of the century. A point of historical interest is that this was the first underground railway to be built on the European continent. The cars first introduced in 1896 were in use until 1973, when they were taken out of circulation after the underground had been completely reconstructed. Today it is 4.5 km (3 m.) long. (The old cars which were in use until 1973 and the history of the underground railway are displayed in a small museum, opening from the Deák tér subway, on an old track of the underground.)

The Hungarian *Transport Museum* (26 Május 1. út, XIV) is nearly a hundred years old, but its collection was almost entirely destroyed during the siege of Budapest in 1945. Since then it has been rebuilt and the collection enriched by new acquisitions. In the museum some valuable models can be found relating to navigation and the railways. Adults and children would spend hours gazing at the rarities of the museum which include the aeroplanes, motorcars, city-transport vehi-

The Danube bank in Pest (Belgrád rakpart)

cles of more than 50 years ago. A new wing was added in 1987.

The *Foundry Museum* in Bem József utca (in Buda) presents interesting relics of the history of manufacture. From the middle of the nineteenth century to the 1940s there was an actual foundry in the building. Here, in the great age of railways, Abraham Ganz, who was of Swiss origin, manufactured cast steel wheels. The museum presents foundry tools and casting moulds, and one of the blast-furnaces has been left intact. The ancient tools of other Hungarian foundries have also been added to the collection; thus the museum gives an overall picture of the history of the iron industry in Hungary.

Those who are interested in technological curiosities will find it worthwhile to visit the *Fire Service Museum* (Martinovics tér, X) which presents, in addition to the hand-appliances of the former voluntary firemen, many curios from the first years of the professional fire-brigades, such as a horse-cart, a hand-pump and an extension ladder.

Interesting relics of electrical lighting in Budapest, which dates back to 1909, can be seen in an old transformer house at the *Museum of Hungarian Electrotechnology* (21 Kazinczy utca, VIII).

The *Postal Services Museum* (3 Népköztársaság útja, VI) also presents interesting technical relics, e.g. an old hand-operated telephone exchange and the first wireless transmitter. The collection also commemorates *Tivadar Puskás* who, after working for a time with Edison, came home to Budapest in the 1900s and set up a "telephonograph" network. In their wired apparatuses, subscribers could regularly hear the news and even transmissions of theatrical or opera performances.

In the *Planetarium* (Népliget, X, terminal of trolley-bus 75, Metro station at Könyves Kálmán körút), films about the solar system and the stars are shown daily.

SZENTENDRE, VISEGRÁD, ESZTERGOM, NAGYMAROS, VÁC

We warmly recommend a whole day's excursion to the beautiful region to the north of Budapest known as the "Danube Bend"; it is here that the great river forces its way through the mountains in a narrow horse-shoe curve to reach the Great Hungarian Plain. This region is closely connected with the capital in its history and thus in its monuments. Among its two most important centres are *Szentendre* and *Visegrád*. Szentendre can be reached by the suburban express railway that starts at Batthyány tér in Buda. At Szentendre you will find a bus connection to Visegrád. There is also a direct coach service from the coach terminus in Engels tér and a very pleasant way of travelling is to take the boat starting at the Vigadó tér landing stage. By car you will drive along Road No. 11 (which can be reached from the Buda end of Margaret Bridge via Árpád fejedelem útja and Szentendrei út).

Szentendre is a charming little town with 19,000 inhabitants situated on the side of the Danube 19 kilometres (12 m.) from the capital. The Serbians, who fled here from the Turks, gave the town its present Baroque character in the eighteenth century. The richly-adorned churches, the beautiful houses of former merchants in the centre of the town, and the meandering streets running through the one-time settlement of vine-growers give the place a special atmosphere. This special atmosphere is also due to the fact that although practically no Baroque-style Orthodox churches were built outside Hungary, in this little town alone we find six of them. The collection of the *Museum of Serbian Ecclesiastical History,* the permanent exhibition of *Margit Kovács,* ceramist, the painter *Béla Czóbel's Memorial Museum,* the *Jenő Barcsay Collection,* the *Szentendre Gallery* and the *Ferenczy Museum* are well worth seeing. Every summer an open-air stage is set up on the main square of the town, where classical prose and musical plays of the *commedia dell'arte* type are performed. In a nearby valley an open-air *ethnographical museum* has been set up. The small town, which is particularly beautifully situated, also houses a lively *artists' colony*. The restaurants offer Serbian specialities.

Visegrád is a village and holiday resort with 2,500 inhabitants in the southern part of the Danube Bend, on the site of a former Roman and subsequently a ninth-century Slav settlement. In the mid-fourteenth century the Angevin kings built the citadel and, under its protection, the palace near the Danube, one of the royal seats. Visegrád's golden age was in the reign of King Matthias, the great Renaissance ruler, who in the fifteenth century had a Gothic palace built here and decorated it with Renaissance ornaments. The *palace* contained 350 rooms, several hanging gardens and a red marble fountain. All this was so magnificent that

Szentendre: the steps leading up to the Castle

Szentendre

a contemporary historian, Miklós Oláh, called it a "Paradise on Earth". The palace was greatly damaged during the Turkish siege and slowly fell into ruins. During the work of excavation many relics have come to light: a corridor of the cloister with stone-figured banisters; three sections of the rim of an octagonal Renaissance red marble well representing Hercules and decorated with King Matthias's coat of arms; hanging gardens and ceremonial courts; bathing rooms and the ruins of the chapel. A visit to the ever-growing collec-

Visegrád: the cloister in King Matthias's palace

tion of the *King Matthias Museum* (Mátyás Király Múzeum) in the Solomon's Tower will complete the picture the visitor has formed of the palace. On the hillside south of the palace stands *Solomon's Tower,* the nucleus of the lower fortress system built by King Béla IV in the thirteenth century. This relatively intact five-storey keep is 31 metres (102 ft.) high, its walls are 3.5

metres (11.5 ft.), at the edges up to 8 metres (25 ft.) thick. Only a few windows decorated with early Gothic pillarheads have been cut in the unbroken walls; from these a wonderful view unfolds itself over the Danube Bend. In addition to a permanent exhibition displaying the original relics found in the palace area, temporary ones are also held in the tower.

Along an excellent road a regular coach service will take you up to the ruins of the triangular *citadel*, in which the royal crown of Hungary used to be kept.

From the top of the hill the visitor will be delighted by the extraordinary panorama before his eyes: the curving Danube, the circle of the Pilis mountains, the Börzsöny mountains opposite, and below, the little villages along the river. From the citadel the road continues to the *Nagyvillám* lookout tower, the Silvanus hotel and the tourist hostel.

From Visegrád along the picturesque Danube bank the road takes us to **Esztergom,** where at one time the

Vác: Triumphal Arch

Hungarian kings were crowned; here the ruins of an eleventh–twelfth-century *royal palace and chapel* have been unearthed by archaeologists. A visit to the sixteenth-century *Bakócz chapel* and the *Treasury* of the *nineteenth-century neo-Classical Cathedral* and to the unique collection of the *Christian Museum* nearby will make the excursion to this lovely little Baroque town most rewarding.

From Visegrád a ferry runs to **Nagymaros.** On your way back to Budapest from here it is worthwhile making a stop in **Vác,** a town with 34,000 inhabitants, which, being an old Episcopal See, can boast of some beautiful Baroque monuments. Its medieval and Renaissance buildings were almost completely destroyed during the Turkish occupation. *Vác Cathedral* was built between 1762 and 1772 to the plans of F. A. Pilgram and, later, of Isidore Canevale. The main altarpiece was painted by Maulbertsch. The *bridge over the Gombás stream* is of interest not only because of its Baroque style, but also as the scene of a decisive battle in the 1848–49 War of Independence.

Practical Information

Tourist information in English:
TOURINFORM, 2 Sütő utca, V; tel.: 179-800

HOW TO GET TO BUDAPEST

Budapest is an important junction in international air, rail, road and river traffic, and the centre of the country's railway network.

Budapest's **international airports, Ferihegy I and II,** can be reached from the city centre by bus, which departs at half-hourly intervals from the Engels tér coach terminal, and by car along a slip road branching out from Üllői út.
Information service: Ferihegy I (departure and arrival of foreign airlines): tel.: 570-086; 572-122
Ferihegy II (departure and arrival of MALÉV flights): tel.: 578-768; 578-406
Flight booking by phone: 184-333
Reservation and sale of flight tickets: 19 Apáczai Csere János utca V, tel.: 189-033

Railway stations: Keleti pályaudvar (Eastern Railway Station), Baross tér, VIII (information on international trains tel.: 224-052); Nyugati pályaudvar (Western Railway Station), Marx tér, VI (information on international trains tel.: 315-346); Déli pályaudvar (Southern Railway Station), Alkotás utca, I (information tel.: 558-657).
Railway Service and Information: 35 Népköztársaság útja, VI, tel.: 228-049.

Central Coach Terminal: Engels tér, V (information tel.: 172-966)

137

Népstadion Coach Terminal, Hungária körút–Kerepesi út corner, XIV, tel.: 187-315. (For the region east of the Danube.)
Árpád Bridge Coach Terminal, Árpád-híd, Pest abutment, XIII, tel.: 291-450 (for the Danube Bend)

Persons arriving **by car** are welcome to apply for information or assistance to the National Centre of the Hungarian Automobile Club (4–6 Rómer Flóris utca, II, tel.: 152-040; salvage service tel.: 691-831).

Traffic regulations: The speed limit for motorcars in inhabited areas is 60 km (37 m.) per hour. Sounding the horn in the area of Budapest is prohibited, except to avert immediate danger.

Cars may be hired for a minimum period of one day. Requests for different types of cars can be made at hotels, travel bureaux, or at the airport, in accordance with international regulations, as well as at FŐTAXI, 24–26, Kertész utca, VII, tel.: 221-471. Motorcoaches for groups may be hired at the travel bureaux.

International landing stage: Belgrád rakpart, V (tel.: 181-758)
Scheduled excursion boats start from the landing stage at Vigadó tér to Szentendre, Leányfalu, Vác, Visegrád, Nagymaros, and Esztergom.

CITY TRANSPORT

The Budapest transport network comprises trams, trolley-buses, buses, underground railways, a cogwheel railway, suburban railways and small river boats.

Tramways, trolley-buses and the underground services generally operate from 4 a.m. to midnight, and on some main roads all night. A one-way (yellow) ticket costs 2 forints. Tramway and bus tickets must be bought beforehand at tobacconists' shops or terminals; no tickets are sold on the vehicles themselves. The tickets must be cancelled by inserting them in a machine on the vehicle. For the cogwheel and suburban railways, the Pioneers' Railway, the Teleferic and the small river boats, tickets have to be bought in advance at the booking-office.

Buses generally run from 5 a.m. to 11 p.m., and a one-way (blue) ticket costs 3 Ft. Tickets must be punched as on tramways.

A day ticket valid for all means of public transport costs 24 forints.

Taxi-cabs can be ordered by telephone (FŐTAXI: 222-222; VOLÁNTAXI: 666-666; CITY TAXI: 214-805; BUDATAXI: 294-000; or, at least one hour in advance, 188-888). Cabs may also be found at taxi ranks or on the street if the TAXI sign on top of the cab is illuminated.

TRAVEL OFFICES

IBUSZ
3/c Tanács körút, VII. tel.: 423-140 (main office)
5 Felszabadulás tér, V. tel.: 181-120 (private rooms)
3 Petőfi tér, V. tel.: 185-707 (hotel service)
5 Vörösmarty tér, V. tel.: 172-322 (air and sea tours)
18 József Attila utca, V. tel.: 173-011
Eastern Railway Station, Baross tér, VIII. tel.: 225-429
Western Railway Station, Marx tér, VI. tel.: 491-770
Southern Railway Station, Magyar Jakobinusok tere, XII. tel.: 552-133

Budapest Tourist
5 Roosevelt tér, V. tel.: 173-555
3 Baross tér, VIII. tel.: 336-587
41 Lenin körút, VII. tel.: 426-521

MALÉV AIR TOURS
2 Roosevelt tér, V. tel.: 186-614

Cooptourist
13–15 Kossuth Lajos tér, V. tel.: 121-017
17 Bajcsy-Zsilinszky út, VI. tel.: 310-992
4 Bartók Béla út, XI. tel.: 868-240

Express Travel Bureau for Young People
16 Szabadság tér, V. tel.: 317-777
4 Semmelweis utca, V. tel.: 176-634

Volántourist
11–13 Október 6 utca, V. tel.: 123-410
96 Lenin körút, VI. tel.: 329-393

ACCOMMODATION

In accordance with international practice *hotels* are classified as 5-star, 4-star, 3-star, 2-star and 1-star. Prices usually include breakfast. *Inns* are smaller buildings of a hotel character, mostly with rooms with double beds, and restaurants nearby.
Tourist hostels have rooms with five or more beds and are classified into categories A and B.
Bungalows are individual buildings suitable for accommodating one or two families. Classification: suite, first, second, third class (I, II, III).
Camping sites are classified, depending on the quality of their services, as 4-star, 3-star, 2-star or 1-star.
Paying Guest Service: private rooms and apartments can be rented at the travel agencies.
Accommodation in youth hostels during the summer holiday is handled by the *Express Travel Bureau* for young people (see above).

Hotel Companies
Hungarhotels, 16 Petőfi Sándor utca, V, 1052, tel.: 183-018, telex: 22-4923
Pannonia, 4–6 Kígyó utca, V 1052, tel.: 183-658, telex: 22-6747
Danubius, 8 Martinelli tér, V, tel.: 173-652, telex: 22-6342

Hotels
Cat. *****
Atrium-Hyatt, 2 Roosevelt tér, V, 1051, tel.: 383-000, telex: 22-5485
Hilton, 1–3 Hess András tér, I, 1014, tel.: 751-000, telex: 22-5984
Duna Inter-Continental, 4 Apáczai Csere János utca, V, 1052, tel.: 175-122, telex: 22-5277
Thermal, Margitsziget, XIII, 1138, tel.: 321-100, telex: 22-5463
Cat. ****
Béke Radisson, 97 Lenin körút, VI, 1067, tel.: 323-300, telex: 22-5748
Buda Penta, 41-43 Krisztina körút, I, 1013, tel.: 566-333, telex: 22-5495

Flamenco, 7 Tas vezér utca, XI, 1113, tel.: 252-250, telex: 22-4647
Forum, 12–14 Apáczai Csere János utca, V, 1052, tel.: 178-088, telex: 22-4178
Gellért, 1 Szt. Gellért tér, XI, tel.: 852-200, telex: 22-4363
Grand Hotel Hungária, 88–92 Rákóczi út, VII, 1074, tel.: 229-050, telex: 22-4987
Grand Hotel Ramada, Margitsziget, XIII, 1138, tel.: 111-000, telex: 22-6682
Nemzeti, 4 József körút, VIII, 1088, tel.: 339-160, telex: 22-7710
Novotel, 63-67 Alkotás utca, XII, 1123, tel.: 869-588, telex: 22-5496
Olympia, 40 Eötvös út, XII, 1121, tel.: 568-011, telex: 22-6368
Royal, 49 Lenin körút, VII, 1073, tel.: 533-133, telex: 22-4463
Cat. ***
Aero, 1–3 Ferde utca, IX, 1091, tel.: 274-690, telex: 22-4238
Astoria, 19 Kossuth Lajos utca, V, 1053, tel.: 173-411, telex: 22-4205
Budapest, 47–49 Szilágyi Erzsébet fasor, II, 1026, tel.: 150-230, telex: 22-5125
Emke, 1–3 Akácfa utca, VII, 1072, tel.: 229-812, telex: 22-5789
Erzsébet, 11–15 Károlyi Mihály utca, V, 1053, tel.: 382-111, telex: 22-7497
Európa, 5–7 Hárshegyi út, II, 1021, tel.: 767-122, telex: 22-5113
Expo, 10, Dobi István út, X, 1101, tel.: 842-130, telex: 22-6300
Palace, 43 Rákóczi út, VIII, 1088, tel.: 136-000, telex: 22-4217
Rege, 2 Pálos út, II, 1021, tel.: 767-311, telex: 22-5660
Stadion, 1–3 Ifjúság útja, XIV, 1148, tel.: 631-830, telex: 22-5685
Taverna, 20 Váci utca, V, tel.: 384-998, telex: 22-7294
Volga, 65 Dózsa György út, XIII, 1134, tel.: 290-200, telex: 22-5120
Cat. **
Ifjúság, 1–3 Zivatar utca, II, tel.: 353-331, telex: 22-5102
Metropol, 58 Rákóczi út, VII, 1074, tel.: 421-175, telex: 22-6209
Minol, 45 Batthyány utca, III, 1031, tel.: 800-777, telex: 22-5270

Park, 10 Baross tér, VIII, 1087, tel.: 131-420,
telex: 22-6274
Venus, 2–4 Dósa utca, III, 1031, tel.: 687-252,
telex: 22-5112 (open from April 1 to October 31)
Vörös Csillag, 21 Rege utca, XII, 1121, tel.: 750-522,
telex: 22-5125
Wien, 88–90 Budaörsi út, XI, 1118, tel.: 665-400,
telex: 22-4469
Cat. *
Citadella, Gellérthegy, XI, 1118, tel.: 665-794,
telex: 22-7648
Lido, 67 Nánási út, III, tel.: 886-865, telex: 22-7350
Saturnus, 10 Pillangó utca, XIV, 1149, tel.: 634-353,
telex: 22-7358
Studium, 129 Harmat utca, X, 1104, tel.: 474-147

Inns
Express, 7–9 Beethoven utca, XII, 1126, tel.: 753-082,
telex: 22-4510
Rosella, 21 Gyöngyvirág út XII, 1125, tel.: 150-576
Strand, 3 Pusztakúti út, 1038, Csillaghegy, tel.: 671-999, telex: 22-4482 (open from April to October)
Sport, 9 Üdülő utca, II, 1021
Trio, 20/d Ördögorom út, XI, 1112, tel.: 865-742 (open April to October)
Unicum, 13 Bod Péter utca, XI, 1112

Tourist Hotels
Strand (Cat. A), Csillaghegy, 3 Pusztakúti út, III, 1038, tel.: 671-999 (open from April to October)
Citadella (Cat. B), Gellérthegy, Citadella sétány, XI, 1118, tel.: 665-794

Bungalows
Haladás (Cat. II), 7 Üdülősor, IV, 1044,
tel.: 891-114, telex: 22-7350 (open from April to October)
Konténer (Cat. II), 67 Nánási út, III, 1038, tel.: 886-865, telex: 22-7350
Római fürdő (Cat. II and III), 189 Szentendrei út, III, 1031, tel.: 686-260, telex: 22-5112 (open from May 1 to December 31)
Strand (Cat. suite, II, III), Csillaghegy, 3 Pusztakúti út, III, 1038, tel.: 671-999, telex: 22-4482 (open from April to October)
Vörös Csillag (Cat. suite and II), 21 Rege utca, XII, 1021, tel.: 166-404, telex: 22-5125

Camping Sites
Expo (Cat. *), 10 Dobi István út, X, 1101, tel.: 470-990
Hárshegyi (Cat. ***), 5–7 Hárshegyi út, II, 1021, tel.: 151-482, telex: 22-5113 (open from April to October)
Metro Tenisz (Cat. ***), 222 Csömöri út, XVI, 1162, tel.: 638-505 (open from April to October)
Római fürdő (Cat. ***), 189 Szentendrei út, III, 1031, tel.: 686-260, telex: 22-5112
Rózsakert (Cat ***), 7 Pilisi utca, X, 1106
Tündérhegyi (Cat. **), 8 Szilassy út, XII, 1121
Zugligeti Niche (Cat. ***), 101 Zugligeti út, XII, 1121

HUNGARIAN CUISINE

The world-famous Hungarian art of cooking developed under Serbian, Italian and French influence. A characteristic feature of the richly spiced, savoury Hungarian dishes is the generous use of lard, red pepper and sour cream. Some specialities are a must: *bográcsgulyás* (goulash cooked in a stew pot on an open fire), *paprikás csirke* (paprika chicken), *töltött káposzta* (stuffed cabbage), *erdélyi fatányéros* (mixed grill served on a wooden platter), *rablóhús* (pork in brochette), *házi disznótoros* (pig-killing feast consisting of roast pork, sausages, white and black pudding), *halászlé* (fish soup), Balaton *fogas* (pike-perch), or among noodles and cakes, *túrós csusza* (firmly kneaded dough mixed with curd cheese and topped with cracklings and sour cream), *rétes* (strudel), *vargabéles* (a soft sweet spongecake made with curd and flavoured with vanilla and raisins) and the different varieties of *palacsinta* (pancakes).

The famous, but fiery, Hungarian cherry and apricot brandies *(cseresznyepálinka* and *barackpálinka)* must be mentioned. There is a great variety of Hungarian wines. Very popular are the white wines of the Balaton region *(Szürkebarát, Badacsonyi kéknyelű, Balatonfüredi Rizling, Szentgyörgyhegyi Rizling, Csopaki Rizling)*. World-famous are the different types of wine grown on the Tokaj mountains, to mention a few, *Tokaji Hárslevelű, Tokaji Szamorodni, Tokaji Aszú.* The white and red wines of Eger are also well-known: *Egri leányka, Egri bikavér* (Bull's Blood), *Medoc Noir,* and so are those of Sopron and Southern Hungary, for instance the *red wine of Szekszárd.*

Restaurants can be found in every hotel. Some additional ones, as well as **taverns, pastry-shops and snack-bars** are listed below.

In the Castle District and its neighbourhood
Alabárdos, 2 Országház utca, I.
Lovely medieval rooms; Hungarian specialities
Fehér Galamb, 9–11 Szentháromság utca, I.
Fortuna, 4 Hess András tér, I.
Gothic rooms; medieval wine cellars; gipsy music; dance music
Márványmenyasszony, 6 Márvány utca, I.
Characteristically Hungarian; gipsy music; pleasant garden restaurant in the summer
Pest-Buda, 3 Fortuna utca, I.
Régi Országház, 17 Országház utca, I.
Hungarian-style furnishing; medieval wine cellar; gipsy music

In other districts of Buda
Citadella restaurant and tavern, Gellért Hill, XI.
Hungarian restaurant in old casemates; gipsy music.
Ezüst Ponty, 64 Németvölgyi út, XII. Small restaurant with pleasant atmosphere
Kerék, 103 Bécsi út, III.
Inn-type restaurant; accordion (Schrammel) music
Margit-kert, 15 Margit utca, II.
Pleasant little restaurant, in the summer with garden
Postakocsi, 2 Fő tér, III.
Pleasant dining-room in a Baroque building
Vasmacska, 3–5 Laktanya utca, III.
Vadrózsa, 15 Pentelei M. utca, II. Restaurant with outdoor eating

In the Inner City
Apostolok, 4–6 Kígyó utca, V.
Kárpátia, 4–8 Károlyi Mihály utca, V.
Mátyás Pince, 7 Március 15. tér, V. Gipsy music
Pilvax, Pilvax-köz, V.
Rézkakas, 3 Veres Pálné utca, V. No music
Százéves, 2 Pesti Barnabás utca, V.

In other parts of Pest
Dunapark, 38 Pozsonyi út, XIII.
Gundel, 2 Állatkerti körút, XIV.
Traditional, fashionable restaurant with several rooms.
Hungária, 9–11 Lenin körút, VII.
Thököly, 80 Thököly út, XIV.

Restaurants serving special dishes
Aranyszarvas, 1 Szarvas tér, I.
Wild game specialities
Bajkál, 1 Semmelweis utca, V.
Russian specialities
Berlin, 13 Szent István körút, V.
German specialities
Étoile, 4 Pozsonyi út, XIII. French specialities
Hanna, 35 Dob utca, VII. Kosher food
Havanna 21 Bajcsy-Zsilinszky út, VI. Cuban cuisine
Hársfa, 132 Vörös Hadsereg útja, II.
Wild game specialities; garden restaurant in summer
Japán Restaurant, 4–6 Luther utca, VIII.
Megyeri Csárda, 192 Váci út, IV.
Hungarian-style inn with gipsy music
Paksi Halászcsárda, 14 Mártírok útja, II.
Fish specialities
Sipos Halászkert, 6 Fő tér, III. Fish restaurant
Szecsuán, Roosevelt tér, V, Chinese cuisine
Szeged, 1 Bartók Béla út, XI.
Tisza region fish specialities
Szófia, 13–15 Kossuth Lajos tér, V.
Bulgarian specialities
Tabáni Kakas, 27 Attila út, I.
Poultry specialities; accordion (Schrammel) music
Thököly, 80 Thököly út, XIV.
Transylvanian specialities
Vörös Sárkány, 80 Népköztársaság útja, VI.
Chinese cuisine

Taverns and beer houses
Alabárdos pince, 2 Országház utca, I.
Bajor sörbár, 7 Károlyi Mihály utca, V.
Bécsi söröző, 8 Eötvös Loránd utca, V.
In the caves below Buda Castle
Borkatakomba, 64 Nagytétényi út, XXII.
Wine cellar cut in the hillside
Fortuna pince, 4 Hess András tér, I.
In old cellars of Buda Castle
Háry borozó, 30 Bródy Sándor utca, VIII.
Harp music
Kaltenberg Söröző, 30–36 Kinizsi utca, IX.
Pepita Oroszlán, 40 Váci utca, V.
Radeberger Söröző, 16 Hídfő utca, III.
Régi Országház pince, 17 Országház utca, I.
In medieval cellars; gipsy music

Rondella Borozó, 4 Régiposta utca, V.
Vigadó Söröző, 2 Vigadó tér, V.

Snack-bars
Mézes Mackó, 4–6 Kígyó utca, V.
City-Grill, 6 Tolbuhin körút, V.
20 Váci utca, V.
13 Szt. István körút, V.
70 Bajcsy-Zsilinszky út, VI.
3 Jászai Mari tér, XIII.
McDonald's, 10 Régiposta utca, V.

Pastry-shops and espressos
Angelika, 7 Batthyány tér, I.
Anna, 7 Váci utca, V.
Gerbeaud, 6 Vörösmarty tér, V.
Hauer, 49 Rákóczi út, VIII.
Jégbüfé, 2 Petőfi Sándor utca, V.
Korona, 16 Dísz tér, I.
Lukács, 70 Népköztársaság útja, VI.
Művész, 29 Népköztársaság útja, VI.

Night-clubs
In addition to those listed below, there are night-clubs or bars in most of the hotels.
Casanova, 4 Batthyány tér, II.
Fortuna bár, 4 Hess András tér, I. Dance music
Hungária bár, 9–11 Lenin körút, VII. Dance music
Lido, 5 Szabadsajtó út, V.
Maxim, 3 Akácfa utca, VII. Cabaret programme
Moulin Rouge, 71 Nagymező utca, VI. Show;
Pipacs, 5 Aranykéz utca, V.

THEATRES, CONCERT HALLS AND OTHER PLACES OF ENTERTAINMENT

Theatrical performances usually start at 7, concerts at 7.30 p.m. Tickets can be purchased at the box-offices of the theatres and the Academy of Music, or in advance at the Central Theatre Ticket Agency (*Színházak Központi Jegyirodája*, 18 Népköztársaság útja, VI; 3 Moszkva tér, II; 29–33 Lenin körút, VII), at the Concert Agency (*Hangversenyjegy-iroda*, 1 Vörösmarty tér, V) or from the hotel hostesses.

Theatres

Állami Bábszínház (State Puppet Theatre), 69 Népköztársaság útja, VI, and 10 Jókai tér, VI; programmes for adults and children.
Arany János Színház (János Arany Theatre), 35 Paulay Ede utca, VI.
Egyetemi Színpad (University Theatre), 1 Pesti Barnabás utca, V.
Erkel Színház (Erkel Opera Theatre), 30 Köztársaság tér, VIII; opera performances, concerts.
Fővárosi Operettszínház (Municipal Operetta Theatre), 17 Nagymező utca, VI.
Játékszín (Playhouse), 106 Lenin körút, VI.
József Attila Színház (József Attila Theatre), 63 Váci út, XIII.
Katona József Színház (Katona József Theatre), 6 Petőfi Sándor utca, V.
Madách Színház (Madách Theatre), 29–33 Lenin körút, VII.
Madách Kamaraszínház (Madách Studio Theatre), 6 Madách tér, VII.
Mikroszkóp Színpad (Microscope Theatre), 22–24 Nagymező utca, VI.
Nemzeti Színház (National Theatre), 2 Hevesi Sándor tér, VII.
Ódry Színpad (Ódry Theatre), 2/c Vas utca, VIII.
Operaház (Opera House), 22 Népköztársaság útja, VI.
Pesti Színház (Pest Theatre), 9 Váci utca, V.
Radnóti Színpad (Radnóti Literary Theatre), 11 Nagymező utca, VI.
Thália Színház (Thalia Theatre), 22–24 Nagymező utca, VI.
Várszínház (Castle Theatre), 2 Színház utca, I.
Vidám Színpad (Gaiety Stage, Political Cabaret) and
Vígszínház (Comedy Theatre), 14 Szt. István körút, XIII.

Concert halls

Zeneakadémia (Academy of Music), 8 Liszt Ferenc tér, VI.
Vigadó, Vigadó tér, V.
Budapest Kongresszusi Központ (Budapest Convention Centre) 1–3 Jagelló út, XII.
Liszt Ferenc Kamaraterem, 35 Vörösmarty utca, VI.

Open-air theatres
Budai Parkszínpad (Open-Air Theatre of Buda), Kosztolányi Dezső tér, XI.
Margitszigeti Szabadtéri Színpad (Open-Air Theatre on Margaret Island), XIII.
Városmajori Szabadtéri Színpad (Open-Air Theatre in the Városmajor), XII.
Zenélő Udvar (Music Court), 62 Úri utca, I.
Zichy kastély 1 Fő tér, III. Óbuda

Other places of entertainment
Amusement Park (Vidám Park), 14–16 Állatkerti körút, City Park, XIV.
Municipal Circus (Fővárosi Nagycirkusz), 7 Állatkerti körút, City Park, XIV.
Planetarium, at the corner of Üllői út and Könyves Kálmán körút
The Zoological and Botanical Gardens of Budapest (Budapesti Állat- és Növénykert), 8–10 Állatkerti körút, City Park, XIV.

MUSEUMS, EXHIBITIONS

Most museums are open on all days of the week from 10 a.m. to 6 p.m., except Monday.

Exhibitions on city history
Aquincum Museum (Aquincumi Múzeum), 139 Szentendrei út, III. Open from 15 April to 1 November.
Roman Bath at Flórián tér (Flórián téri római katonai fürdő), Flórián tér, III.
Budapest History Museum, Castle Museum (Budapesti Történeti Múzeum, Vármúzeum), Royal Palace of Buda, E wing.
Kiscelli Museum, 108 Kiscelli út, III. The history of Budapest from 1686. Works of art depicting the capital.
The Tomb of Gül Baba, 14 Mecset utca, II. Open from 10 a.m. to 2 p.m., on Saturday to 6 p.m.

National history collections
Hungarian National Museum (Magyar Nemzeti Múzeum), 14–16 Múzeum körút, VIII.
Museum of the Hungarian Working-Class Movement (Magyar Munkásmozgalmi Múzeum), Royal Palace of Buda, A wing.
War History Museum (Hadtörténeti Múzeum), 40 Tóth Árpád sétány, I. Open 9 a.m.–5 p.m.

Jewish Religious and Historic Collection (Országos Zsidó Vallási és Történeti Múzeum), 2 Dohány utca, VII. Open from 15 April to 15 October on Monday and Thursday from 2 p.m. to 6 p.m., on Tuesday, Friday and Sunday from 10 a.m. to 1 p.m.
Medieval Jewish Prayer Hall (Középkori Zsidó Imaház), 26 Táncsics Mihály utca, I. Open on Tuesday, Wednesday, Thursday and Friday from 10 a.m. to 2 p.m. On Saturday and Sunday from 10 a.m. to 6 p.m.
Lutheran National Museum (Evangélikus Országos Múzeum), 4 Deák tér, V.

Art and literary collections
Museum of Fine Arts (Szépművészeti Múzeum), 41 Dózsa György út, XIV.
Hungarian National Gallery (Magyar Nemzeti Galéria), Royal Palace of Buda, B–C–D wings.
Ethnographical Museum (Néprajzi Múzeum), 12 Kossuth Lajos tér, V.
Museum of Applied Arts (Iparművészeti Múzeum), 33–37 Üllői út, IX. Open 10 a.m.–6 p.m.
Museum of Music History (Zenetörténeti Múzeum), 7 Táncsics Mihály utca, I.
Nagytétény Castle Museum (Nagytétényi Kastélymúzeum), 9 Csókási Pál utca, Nagytétény XXII. Exhibition of Hungarian furniture.
Petőfi Literary Museum (Petőfi Irodalmi Múzeum), 16 Károlyi Mihály utca, V.
Chinese Museum (Kína Múzeum), 12 Gorkij fasor, VI.
Museum of Eastern Asiatic Art (Hopp Ferenc Kelet-Ázsiai Múzeum), 103 Népköztársaság útja, VI.
Gizi Bajor Actors' Museum (Bajor Gizi Színészmúzeum), 16 Stromfeld Aurél utca, XII.
Collection of Ecclesiastical Art in Matthias Church (Church of Our Lady) (Mátyás-templom Egyházművészeti Gyűjteménye), 1 Szentháromság tér, I. Open daily 9 a.m.–7 p.m.

Scientific, technical and other collections
Museum of Natural Sciences (Természettudományi Múzeum), accommodated in the Hungarian National Museum (14–16 Múzeum körút, VIII).
Museum of Agriculture (Mezőgazdasági Múzeum), Városliget, XIV, Vajdahunyad Castle on Széchenyi Island. Plant cultivation, animal husbandry and forestry exhibitions.

Transport Museum (Közlekedési Múzeum), 26 Május 1. út, XIV. Ancient means of transport, models and scale models.
Foundry Museum (Öntödei Múzeum), 20 Bem József utca, II.
Semmelweis Museum of Medical History (Semmelweis Orvostörténeti Múzeum), 1–3 Apród utca, I. Open 10 a.m.–6 p.m.
Pharmaceutical Museum (Arany Sas Patikamúzeum), 18 Tárnok utca, I.
Museum of Catering and Trade (Kereskedelmi és Vendéglátóipari Múzeum), 4 Fortuna utca, I.
Museum of Physical Education and Sports (Testnevelési és Sportmúzeum), 3 Dózsa György út, XIV.
Philatelic Museum (Bélyegmúzeum), 47 Hársfa utca, VII. Open 10 a.m.–4 p.m. on Wednesdays, 10 a.m.–3 p.m. on Saturdays, 10 a.m.–2 p.m. on Sundays.
Postal Services Museum (Postamúzeum), 3 Népköztársaság útja, VI.
Museum of the Fire Service (Tűzoltó Múzeum), 12 Martinovics tér, X. Open 10 a.m.–6 p.m. on Wednesdays and Fridays, 10 a.m.–2 p.m. on Sundays.
Underground Railway Museum (Földalatti Vasút Múzeum), in the Deák tér subway, V.

Exhibition halls
Art Gallery (Műcsarnok), 37 Dózsa György út, XIV.
Csók István Gallery, 25 Váci utca, V.
Csontváry Showroom, 1 Vörösmarty tér, V.
Derkovits Gyula Showroom, 63 Lenin körút, VI.
Dürer Showroom, 52 Bajcsy-Zsilinszky út, V.
Ernst Museum, 8 Nagymező utca, VI.
Fényes Adolf Showroom, 30 Rákóczi út, VII.
Mednyánszky Showroom, 26 Tanács körút, V.
Paál László Showroom, 57/b Rákóczi út, VIII.
Pór Bertalan Showroom, 70 József körút, VIII.
Dorottya Street Showroom, 8 Dorottya utca, V.
Studió Gallery, 52 Bajcsy-Zsilinszky út, V.
Photo Art Gallery, 7 Váci utca, V.
Gulácsy Gallery, 4 Fürj utca, XII.
Helikon Gallery, 8 Eötvös Loránd utca, V.
Qualitas Gallery, 2 Bécsi utca, V.
Castle Theatre Gallery, 1–3 Színház utca, I.
Vigadó Gallery, 2 Vigadó tér, V.

SPORTS

Népstadion (People's Stadium), 3–5 Istvánmezei út, XIV.
Budapest Sportcsarnok (Budapest Sports Hall), 48–52 Hungária körút, XIV.
Nemzeti Sportcsarnok (National Sports Hall), 1–3 Istvánmezei út, XIV.
Kisstadion (Little Stadium), Rövid utca, XIV.
Műjégpálya (Artificial Skating Rink), Népstadion út, City Park, XIV.
Nemzeti Lovarda (National Riding Hall), 7 Kerepesi út, VIII.
Ügetőpálya (Trotting Race Course), 9 Kerepesi út, VIII.
Galopp pálya (Galloping Race Course), 2 Dobi István út, X.
Komjádi Béla Sportuszoda (Béla Komjádi Sports Swimming Pool), 2–4, Komjádi Béla utca, III.
Hajós Alfréd Sportuszoda (Alfréd Hajós Sports Swimming Pool), Margaret Island, XIII.
Teniszstadion (Tennis Stadium), Margaret Island, XIII.

POSTAL SERVICES

Central Post Office (No. 4): 18 Városház utca, V.
Telegram and telephone service: 17–19 Petőfi Sándor utca, V.
Round the clock service: Post Office No. 62, near the Western Railway Station (105 Lenin körút, VI) and No. 72, at the Eastern Railway Station (1 Verseny utca, VII). Letters mailed "Poste Restante" should bear the number of the post office, e.g. 1364 Budapest, Poste Restante. All postal material must bear the postal code number.
Local calls from telephone-booths can be made with a two-forint piece.
Long-distance calls to some inland towns can be made direct by dialling 06 and, after the buzzing sound, the area code and the required phone number. Other long-distance calls can be made by dialling 01 and asking for the town and number required. Trunk-calls *abroad* can be made either direct, by dialling 00 and, after the buzzing sound, the numbers of the country, the town and the station, or by dialling 09 and asking for the required connection. *Telephone Information Service* on

telephone numbers in Hungary and abroad in English, French, German and Russian: 186-977.

NEWSPAPERS, JOURNALS

Major foreign dailies can be bought in hotels and at some larger newspaper kiosks. Hungarian foreign-language papers are the *Daily News-Neueste Nachrichten* (daily), *Budapester Rundschau* (weekly), *Hungarian Digest* and *The New Hungarian Quarterly*. *Coming Events in Budapest* appears monthly in Hungarian, German, English and French and gives information about the month's cultural events and other entertainment.

SHOPPING

Shops selling consumer goods are open in the Inner City from 10 a.m. to 6 p.m., on the Great Boulevard and on Rákóczi út generally from 10 a.m. to 7 p.m., on Thursdays to 8 p.m. *Department stores* are usually open from 9 a.m. to 7 p.m., and the majority of *food* and fruit shops from 7 a.m. to 8 p.m. Shops selling consumer goods generally *close on Saturdays* at 1 p.m. On *Sundays and holidays* the Supermarket of the Sugár Department Store (Örs vezér tere, XIV. until 1 p.m.) and some sweet shops, tobacconists', liquor shops and florists are open.

The majority of *hairdressing salons* and *barber's shops* are open from 7 a.m. to 9 p.m., on Saturday to 4 p.m. The larger ones also provide beauty treatment and pedicure. All shops (with the exception of those just mentioned) and all department stores are *closed on Sundays* as well as on the *official holidays:* 1 January, 4 April (Liberation Day), Easter Monday, 1 May, 20 August (Constitution Day), 7 November (Anniversary of the Great October Socialist Revolution), 25 and 26 December.

Department stores
Corvin, 1–2 Blaha Lujza tér, VIII.
Csillag, 20–22 Rákóczi út, VII. (ladies' wear)
Divatcsarnok, 41 Népköztársaság útja, VI.
Flórián, Flórián tér, III.
Városkapu Üzletház, Kálvin tér, IX. (hardware goods)
Lottó, 36 Rákóczi út, VII.
Luxus, 3 Vörösmarty tér, V.

Otthon, 74–76 Rákóczi út, VII. (household articles)
Skála, 6–10 Schönherz Zoltán út, XI.
Skála Metro, Marx tér, VI.
Skála Sprint, 93–103 Lajos utca, III.
Sugár, Örs vezér tere, XIV.
Úttörő és Ifjúsági, 19 Kossuth Lajos utca, V.
Verseny, 12 Rákóczi út, VII. (men's wear)

Folk art shops
34 Mártírok útja, II.
14 Váci utca, V.
2 Kossuth Lajos utca, V.
5 Kálvin tér, V.
12 Régiposta utca, V.
5 Lenin körút, VII.
32 Rákóczi út, VII.
50 Bartók Béla út, XI.
26 Szent István körút, XIII.

Antique shops (selling goods on commission)
3 Felszabadulás tér, V. (furnishings, paintings, china)
5 Felszabadulás tér, V. (carpets)
1–3 Kossuth Lajos utca, V. (furniture, antiques, china)
3 Szent István körút, XIII. (furniture, paintings)
3 Hess András tér, I. (antiques)

Gift shops
4 Kígyó utca, V.
7 József nádor tér, V.
2 Vörösmarty tér, V.
76 Lenin körút, VI.
44 Lenin körút, VII.
9 Váci utca, V.
30 Váci utca, V.
6 Kossuth Lajos utca, V.
8 Petőfi Sándor utca, V.
30 Rákóczi út, VII.
38 Rákóczi út, VII.
52 Rákóczi út, VII.

Record shops
1 Vörösmarty tér, V.
8 Kossuth Lajos utca, V.
42–44 Lenin körút, VII.
5 Martinelli tér, V.
5 Lenin körút, VI.
60 Rákóczi út, VII.

Some bookshops
3 Hess András tér, I. (books in foreign languages)
22 Váci utca, V. (Academy Bookshop; scientific works in foreign languages)
32 Váci utca, V. (books in foreign languages)
33 Váci utca, V. (Gorky Bookshop; books in foreign languages)
2–4 Petőfi Sándor utca, V. (Paris Arcades) (books in foreign languages, guide-books, maps)
15 Múzeum körút, V. (central second-hand bookshop)
5 Martinelli tér, V. (music shop)
2 Népköztársaság útja, VI. (second-hand bookshop)

14 Rákóczi út, VII. (book department store)
52 Lenin körút, VII. (Erkel music shop)

Intertourist shops
(antiquities, works of art, gifts; for convertible currency only)
5 Kígyó utca, V. (china, goldsmith's work, folk art objects)
27 Népköztársaság útja, VI. (carpets, crystal glass, china)
43 Népköztársaság útja, VI. (period furniture, paintings, statuary)
Also in hotels.

Major sports goods shops
Camping Department Store, 26 Váci utca, V.
Fishing gear, 57 Lenin körút, VI.
Diana hunting equipment, on the corner of Harmincad utca and József nádor tér, V.

Messenger service (Boy-szolgálat), 20 Bajcsy-Zsilinszky út, V. (Delivery of parcels to a given address; tel.: 323–523.)
The department stores will also arrange delivery.

SOME IMPORTANT ADDRESSES

Budapest Police Headquarters (Budapesti Rendőrfőkapitányság), 16–18 Deák Ferenc utca, V. tel.: 123-456
Ministry of Foreign Affairs (Külügyminisztérium), 47 Bem rakpart, II. tel.: 568-000
Hungarian Chamber of Commerce (Magyar Kereskedelmi Kamara), 6–8 Kossuth tér, V. tel.: 314-155
Hungarian Automobile Club (Magyar Autóklub), 4–6 Rómer Flóris utca, II. International Information Service, tel.: 152-040
Hungarian Camping and Caravanning Club,
11 Múzeum utca, VIII. tel.: 141-880
World Federation of Hungarians (Magyarok Világszövetsége), 15 Benczúr utca, VI. tel.: 225-405
Lost Property Offices 18 Akácfa utca, VII (for trams, buses and trolley-buses). tel.: 226-613
5 Engels tér, V. tel.: 174-961
Ambulance, tel.: 04
Fire-guards, tel.: 05
Police, tel.: 07

154